MW01242107

ISBN: 9781973473138

Also available in Digital book(s) (epub and mobi) produced by Booknook.biz.

Foreword

The influencer economy is currently the *wild frontier* of Internet Marketing.

You hear this cliché in about every marketing channel at every marketing conference.

However, influencer marketing has the real feel of the Wild West. Both the good and bad. Influencers are still figuring out all the ways they can make money and exert influence from the platforms, and marketers are still pretty basic with their approach to how to leverage these influencers.

The untamed nature of this space is evident because it is yet to be fully embraced, properly regulated, or precisely measured.

Some marketers will throw up their arms and scream "LIES!"

Calm down and take a few selfies with your sushi.

Major agencies have only scratched the surface with influencer campaigns, focusing mostly on high visibility targets. Paying a Kardashian seven figures to push a product isn't exactly cutting-edge marketing. Wilford Brimley has been pitching me diabetes products since the 80s.

Or maybe that was oatmeal?

Regardless, while the FCC has rules on how advertising with influencers should work, not all platforms or influencers play by the rules. Policing the system is almost impossible, simply relying on making examples of the most visible players or one-off cases.

For agencies and marketers, while basic reporting can be backed out to traffic, attributing influence to a final sale takes real analytical prowess that not every marketer has. Analytics packages simply don't accurately track attribution from the original sources at the epicenter of a viral phenomenon. Analytics packages that do help you grade third party attribution and spread need to be tied to onpage analytics, and, in some cases, offsite sales.

So, we have ourselves a Wild West landscape in the influencer world. In these open rolling lands o' plenty dotted with thriving herds of gaming Youtubers and wagon trains of Instagram models, a smart marketer can stake claim to a fortune. The land grab is happening now, and the best stretches of land may not be where you think they are.

If you want to see the real power the influencers yield, the best case study is the 2016 Presidential Campaigns.

FAKE NEWS!

You can't hear this phrase without it playing in your head in Donald Trump's voice. It has become his go-to term when discussing mainstream media organizations.

However, before Trump appropriated the term, it was a concept brought into the spotlight when people noticed the wild circulation of obviously faked news articles on Facebook and other platforms.

- "FBI AGENT SUSPECTED IN HILLARY EMAIL LEAKS FOUND DEAD IN APPARENT MURDER-SUICIDE"
- "BREAKING: Pope Francis Just Backed Trump, Released Incredible Statement Why"
- "Doctor Who Treated Hillary's Blood Clots Found Dead"

These are real titles from actual Fake News that spread in 2016.

While some would speculate that these stories were put out to help or hurt one candidate, it is hard to speculate whether that is the reason or pure greed. These articles went viral, which means lots of clicks and lots of ad traffic. Maybe it was a mix. The reason isn't important for our conversation. The methodology of how these articles spread is what is of chief importance.

Facebook and social platforms were never meant to be our source for news and information. While the rise of the citizen journalist can be credited with bringing light to many dark corners of this world, the reality is that citizens know very little about true journalism. The core of true journalism is to distinguish fact from fiction and report on details that have been verified. Your Grandma Betty has very different editorial controls than the Washington Post; however, social media outlets give her just as large of an audience.

The fake news issue is a real problem with no real solution. Consider:

- 62 percent of US adults get news on social media.
- The most popular fake news stories were more widely shared on Facebook than the most popular mainstream news stories.
- Many people who see fake news stories report that they believe them.
- The most discussed fake news stories tended to favor Donald Trump over Hillary.

THE BOT WAR OF 2016

The influencer war of the 2016 election was the first time that non-marketers and technically skilled users began to discuss the role of "bots" in social media.

Bots are essentially artificial social media accounts that are usually automated or a mix of automation and human interaction. The "bots" are fake people on platforms designed to connect real people.

The bot war was fought on both sides, and based on data and intelligence also internationally by countries like Russia looking to influence our population.

The influence of these bots taught us a lot about how influence actually works online. While top-notch influencers with a huge following can have big impacts on amplification, the real power is in amplifying your message with large amounts of influencers that have messages that match their interests. The influence does not need to be about the relationship, but whether the message the influencer sends is something that resonates with the user's preconceived likes and beliefs.

BATTING FOR PERCENTAGE, NOT FOR HOMERUNS

The case study of the 2016 Election shows us that massive wins come from the influence of many small, trusted accounts pushing information.

Viral marketers have largely fallen into the trap that viral success equals having content shared by a single source that amplifies the content. On its face, this concept is true; however, it is not the only route to a big win.

In baseball, a home run with no one on base scores as many points as a single with bases loaded. From a statistical standpoint, the likelihood of a batter hitting a single rather than a home run is based on their overall hitting performance. However, the likelihood of a single can be between 15 to 20x more likely than a homer.

If you are working on a paid influencer campaign with a set budget, do you spend your entire budget on one major social media star sharing your message or 500 lower tier niche targeted influencers? There is no blanketed answer; however, the common group think in Agency Land is the major social media star despite the statistical probability of getting gains from a larger amplification base.

Why?

Mostly because the screen captured Tweet of a major celebrity sharing a message is something a customer can understand and is less likely to question if it fails.

The unclaimed land in the influencer space lies with the masses, and the marketer looking to hit lots of singles can create a data-driven approach to influencer marketing that yields measurable ROI.

AM I AN INFLUENCER?

The simple answer to whether you are an influencer is yes. We are all already influencers; we were influencers before social media was even a construct.

Historically, humans have made decisions and formed opinions based on the decisions and opinions of others. We closely identify with other humans based on cultural or philosophical similarities, and the fact that someone of a similar makeup has approved a service or product sits well with us. This meant your earliest influencers were your family, parents, or caretakers. They exerted influence on you on a daily basis without you having to think about it.

On the next level of the spectrum, Star Power based influencer marketing is no different than the concept of company spokespeople. Companies are looking to leverage the credibility someone has built up with a group on behalf of their brand.

The modern influencer is a tastemaker, and in order to be a tastemaker in the social media world, you need not be a person who has the universal appeal of a Michael Jordan. In fact, if you are an influencer who wants to succeed in building a brand, you should think about going niche.

NICHE TASTES AND NICHE INFLUENCE

Every Saturday I wake up to my sons watching gaming channels on YouTube.

It makes me sad because my nostalgic side longs for the days I would wake up on a Saturday morning, grab a bowl of cereal, and turn on Muppet Babies.

Now my kids are listening to some blue-haired British guy as he plays a game.

The top of the gaming mountain is PewDiePie. He boasts over 56 million subscribers to his YouTube channel, and any video he posts is guaranteed to get millions of views. This is a person whose fame has come from being an expert in a niche; he is not a famous person who has moved over to a niche.

"Well Dave, isn't PewDiePie a home run and not a single?"

Absolutely.

So, look farther down the list for value. All the top 250 gaming personalities on YouTube boast over 2 million subscribers. There are YouTube personalities with hundreds of thousands of subscribers doing video creation full-time. The key is building an audience within a niche where you have a knowledge base and passion.

WHAT YOU WILL LEARN HERE

Joe Sinkwitz, founder of Intellifluence, knows the influencer space better than anyone I have ever met. That doesn't just mean the tip of the iceberg. Joe understands the niche market and even the dirty bot-filled underbelly.

Marketers will learn how to effectively frame, engage in, and monitor their influencer marketing campaigns.

Influencers will learn how to maximize their value. Joe will help guide you into the wilderness and opportunity that still exists in this dynamic space.

Table Of Contents

The Ultimate Guide to Using Influencer Marketing

Prologue

Welcome to what has been over eighteen months of effort. During that time, we compiled data and covered a wide variety of topics related to how a brand or agency could use influencer marketing in its overall marketing mix to increase sales. The culmination of 29 articles is what I now believe to be two very comprehensive guides and a useful book on everything influencer marketing.

For your reading ease this guide is designed in a table of contents format with executive summaries of each piece, allowing you to immediately skip to sections you're most interested in. If you are new to influencer marketing, we recommend starting at the beginning and reading the articles in order. They are as detailed as I could make them and contain supporting information not presented in the executive summaries.

Have questions, comments, or love letters? Please like, share, and comment below. I'll do my best to answer them in a timely manner.

Photo 1.1. Credit: Kimson Doan

CHAPTER 1

What Is Influencer Marketing?

A primer of how influencer marketing came to be, from its roots as word-of-mouth marketing to present-day format. Learn the differences between aspirational, authoritative, and peer influencers, why influencer marketing can be adopted by any B2C or B2B business, and what makes for a successful campaign. Finally, dive into a breakdown into where influencers are most active today, and get our thoughts on the trending direction of influencer marketing as a function of overall digital marketing: hint, up and to the right.

Influencer marketing, as defined by a bunch of old marketers such as ourselves, can be simply stated as having someone tell your story for you. One common example that most people associate with this type of marketing can be seen on television and in movies when an actor uses a specific product, captivating an audience in its amazingness. Personally, I can attest to its power given that I own several Omega watches just like James Bond; I was unfortunately unable to capture his charm through my purchases. I highlight this specific example for two reasons:

1. **Influencer marketing is not native advertising.** The mistake is often assuming that influence exists in the same manner as product placement (a common form of native advertising). While there is an overlap — and in a later chapter, I'll explain in greater detail how to pair the two different types of marketing to create a compulsion for your product — it is the lack of explicit endorsement that in my mind separates native advertising and influencer marketing. The product without a story is native advertising; with the story it becomes influencer marketing.

2. **The other reason I highlight this example is because it is largely out of reach of most businesses.** I highlighted the use of aspirational (that is, celebrity) influence. While it is clearly effective, it isn't even the most effective form of influencer marketing, which I hope to convince you by the end of this book.

WORD OF MOUTH

To understand the concept better, we need to look at its roots. While storytelling is as old as human history itself, the idea was acutely defined in the 1970s by psychologist George Silverman. George was so far ahead of his time that he actually coined the concept initially as "teleconferenced peer influence groups" — what we now refer to as influencer

Photo 1.2. Credit: Alexis Brown

marketing. The idea by George was to build "buzz" to the point of influencing a purchasing decision. On the whole, we like that concept, but we now live in an age of key performance indicators (KPIs), stated goals, and the ability to track and tie a significant amount of purchasing behavior back to those goals. Buzz is fine, but the bottom line is better.

TYPES OF INFLUENCERS

Briefly touched on above in the James Bond example, there are three main types of influencers[1] one can attempt to attract, whose use depends upon one's goals and budget.

1. Aspirational. Aspirational influence, again, is the most "known" of the types as it is what we most recognize as marketing. As a definition, this is the type of influence applied toward someone who is aspiring to be like another person. I wanted to be like James Bond, and I also love fine watches, so Omega it was.

2. Authoritative. Authority is earned in this group. Authoritative influencers are topical experts, whose opinion you trust because you know them to be experts in that realm — James Bond's choice of vodka martini would be a decent example in that, due to his obvious knowledge of the drink and assertiveness in ordering it and correcting the bartender who might accidentally stir his concoction, one might consider him an expert on the topic. If James turned to the camera and stated which specific vodka he prefers and why, chances are sales would increase significantly for that distiller. That endorsement would also be a mix of aspirational and authoritative influence.

3. Peer. The most powerful influence applied is from those whom we believe to be our equals. While we may want what our heroes want and trust what authorities tell us works, we absolutely need to have what our friends and neighbors have. Using James as an example, let us assume that Mr. Bond receives some new gadgets from Q and then is showing off for his fellow MI6 compadres. Do you think they are going to be influenced by a product review from the greatest spy of all time on how he used the gadget on his last mission? No question.

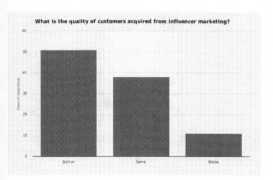

Graphic 1.1: What is the quality of customers acquired from influencer marketing? Source: Tomoson

WHO SHOULD USE INFLUENCER MARKETING?

Any business[2], large or small, can employ the concept. A brand such as Coca Cola might line up a series of positive image celebrities and a pool of several thousand peer level influencers in a global campaign to

[1] Intellifluence (2016). Welcome, influencers Retrieved from https://intellifluence.com/influencers/

[2] Intellifluence. (2016) Hello, brands. Retrieved from https://intellifluence.com/brands

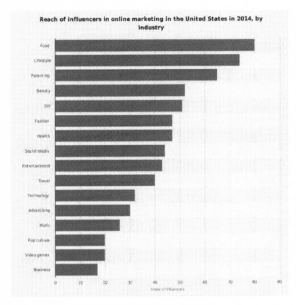

Graphic 1.2: Reach of influencers in online marketing in the United States in 2014, by industry. Source: Various

spread a new advertising message whereas a small e-commerce business is going to see the most results by using a service such as Intellifluence to build a peer influence campaign based on identified buyer personas.[3] The concept even transcends B2C vs. B2B debates; so long as a product or service is for sale, a reviewer can be found to influence a prospective buyer.

According to Tomoson, customers acquired through influencer tactics tend to also be of a higher quality, due to personalized connections. Who am I to argue?

Don't just take my word for it, though, on who should use this marketing concept. A few short years ago, influencer reach was already beginning to extend into all facets of the economy.

WHAT MAKES FOR A SUCCESSFUL CAMPAIGN?

In some cases, a niche blogger community is going to be far more effective than a broader following on Twitter, depending on one's goals. A product reviewer on Amazon for an Amazon-hosted product is going to be more effective than the same person posting

on LinkedIn. What makes for the best campaign is the one that ties both the network and influencer type that best fits a product or service.

B2B campaigns, in our data, have had enormous success on LinkedIn, Facebook, and Twitter when using a mixture of authoritative and peer influencers.

B2C fashion-oriented brands have been skewing toward Instagram, YouTube, Facebook, Pinterest, and Twitter.

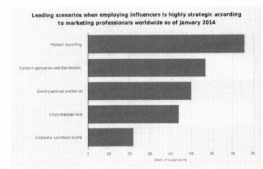

Graphic 1.3: Leading scenarios when employing influencers is highly strategic according to marketing professionals worldwide as of January 2014. Source: Various

[3] Sinkwitz, J. (2016, August 15). How to influence your buyers using content marketing. Retrieved from http://www.copypress.com/blog/how-to-influence-buyers-using-content-marketing/

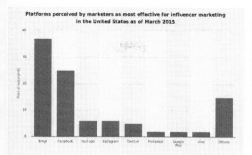

Graphic 1.4: Platforms perceived by marketers as most effective for influencer marketing in the United States as of March 2015. Source: Tomoson

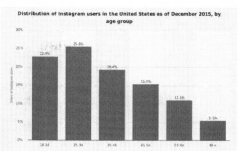

Graphic 1.5: Distribution of Instagram users in the United States as of December 2015, by age group. Source: comScore

B2C services have been using Twitter, YouTube, and Facebook.

Those avenues certainly aren't the only use cases either. Some are using influencers not only to promote products, but also content, activities, and events.

Each business is unique. Where are your potential consumers spending time online? Who influences them? That's where your focus should be. And when in doubt, test. It is very simple to try out different networks and different ranges of reviewers to determine the best way to make influencer marketing work for you.

WHERE ARE INFLUENCERS TODAY?

Any community or group where a person has a potential audience is technically a place where you can find potential influencers. However, not all networks are created equal. Let's dive in to see how the marketplace has been evolving.

The Internet is very fluid in that networks that thrive today might be dying tomorrow. For instance, in 2015, marketing professionals were not focusing nearly as much on Instagram and Pinterest as they are now. Google Plus still held some share (it is virtually dead now according to our data on effectiveness). Our decision to focus initially on blogs, Facebook, YouTube, Instagram, Twitter, Pinterest, and Amazon was deliberate.

Social influence is not just about young adults either. According to comScore, a significant amount of users aligns with the 30- to 40-year age bracket.

As you can see from the following survey of bloggers, the vast majority use social as a means to drive traffic into blog posts. Pairing social with reviews is a winning combination for influencing your end buyer.

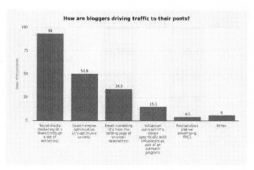

Graphic 1.6. How are bloggers driving traffic to their posts? Source: Orbit Media

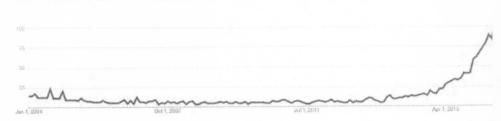

Graphic 1.7: Trends of influencer marketing. Source: Google Trends

IS INFLUENCER MARKETING THE FUTURE OF SOCIAL SELLING?

Without a doubt, influencer marketing as a subject matter is trending as more and more companies are scrambling to figure it out. A recent Google Trends graph explains why.

Whenever the trends have upward slopes like that, you can expect the CMO suite to start asking every agency of record and vendor what is being done to capitalize on the new trend. Why is influencer marketing the future of social selling though?

Spending on social media is expected to increase significantly according to Forrester Research, likely doubling by 2020.

What is it specifically for influencer marketing though?

The biggest leap from the early days of social media to now is that we now have the capacity to tie together sales data with attributed activity that occurs on Twitter, Facebook, and other channels. With this closed loop, we are now able to narrow the focus away from just generating buzz and into creating reviewer campaigns designed to generate more sales with a minimal budget. In that way, influencer marketing is the future.

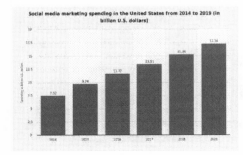

Graphic 1.8: Social media marketing spending in the United States from 2014 to 2019 (in billion U.S. dollars). Source: Forrester Research

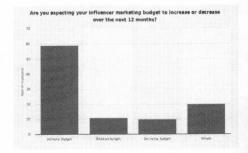

Graphic 1.9: Are you expecting your influencer marketing budget to increase or decrease over the next 12 months? Source: Tomoson

Photo 2.1. Credit: Helloquence

CHAPTER 2

Why Should Influencer Marketing Be Part of Your Strategy?

Should influencer marketing be a part of your plans? Dig into its efficacy compared to other forms of digital marketing and its cost-effective benefits. To understand who to target, included is a primer on how to build a buyer persona based on existing sales data, extrapolating out to a larger set of data using LinkedIn. Next, learn how influencer marketing differs from advertising, how to use it to build brand loyalty, and why it is great for creating promotable content. Finally, grasp the reality that your competitors may already be using influencer marketing or have plans to start.

In Chapter 1, I set out to provide a fairly comprehensive explanation as to "what" influencer marketing is. In this chapter however, I want to cover why it absolutely needs to be a part of your plans. Yes, I'm biased — let's get that out of the way. I'm the CEO of Intellifluence, which specializes in matching up influencers and small businesses to create product reviews that result in sales.

Are you ready for the pitch?

EFFICACY OF PEER INFLUENCER MARKETING VS. OTHER MARKETING TYPES

I'm going to repeat a graph from Tomoson that I used previously. According to the company's research, the quality of customers acquired from influencer marketing was higher.

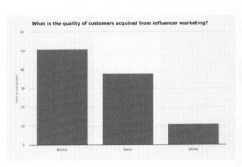

Graphic 2.1: What is the quality of customers acquired from influencer marketing? Source: Tomoson

This sentiment is echoed by Khidr Suleman of PR Week,[4] which showed that peer level influence had the highest level of engagement of any of the Instagram marketing campaigns performed. The efficacy in this case had to do with an increased time commitment of peer influencers (micro-influencers), which created a greater level of engagement due to the closer relationship between influencer and audience. This statement actually ties back around to the Tomoson data because consumers who purchased based on peer influence will churn less frequently than those responding to a non-personalized, non-tribe oriented marketing campaign — the sense of unity and belonging as a psychological trigger has been activated. Like any consumer, if the product and service offered has issues, you can't expect to keep them engaged and happy, but holding all other variables equal, the efficacy of peer influence has a noticeable edge due simply to a lower expected churn rate and higher repeat purchase rate.

IS INFLUENCER MARKETING COST EFFECTIVE?

Efficacy of spend would seem to indicate then that these types of marketing campaigns are going to be inherently cost-effective from a ROI perspective, but it gets better. Since the cost to acquire peer (or micro-influencers, if you prefer) is substantially less expensive than hiring a celebrity, one is able to iterate faster and at a lower market fit cost using traditional A/B testing methods. Using peer influencers as a test bed can actually help you figure out your ideal buyer personas quicker, which can then be used in any of your other marketing plans.

---

[4] Suleman, K. (2016, February 24). Has your agency been using Instagram influencers wrong? Retrieved from http://www.prweek.com/article/1384456/agency-using-instagram-influencers-wrong

HOW TO DETERMINE BUYER PERSONAS

I covered how to build content marketing plans to influence buyers[5] and how to use influence to drive your content marketing,[6] both of which involved understanding the buyer persona. Here's a not-very-quick way to determine some possibilities:

1. Take your last 100 customers (or less — you just need to have "some" data in order to test).

2. Research each customer's social profiles. I used to recommend Vibeapp, but it was purchased by Fullcontact recently, so you might need to use a tool like that if you don't already have your customers' social profiles.

3. For each customer, who does this person aspire to be? Who are the heroes being followed, regardless of subject matter expertise? These answers can be figured out by sorting on raw follower count—the aspirational influencers tend to have larger counts relative to the normal population.

4. Who influences the customer on your particular subject matter? This answer can be more difficult to determine sometimes, but across a handful of customers you might find one or two clearly authoritative figures who are experts in your field or are at least perceived as experts.

5. Who are your customers' peers? This item is the easiest piece, thanks to tools like LinkedIn Sales Navigator. Plug in each of your customers and look at first-level connections and start drawing comparisons.

6. Iterate. For the large lists of peers you've gathered, you'll now need their social profiles. As you cycle through, start looking for patterns on who is also following the same celebrities and authority figures. Pull each of these individuals into a separate worksheet.

7. On the filtered worksheet, you probably have a fairly large number of peers who seem to be influenced by the same celebrities and authority figures. It was exhausting, but this data is actually a targeted buying list if you're so inclined to reach out directly. It is also data you can finally use to build your buyer persona. What are the ages, genders, professions, socioeconomic factors, and interests? You'll likely be able to segment these individuals into rough groups that now represent who is more inclined to purchase what you're selling than a random internet user.

---

[5] Sinkwitz, J. (2016, August 15). How to influence your buyers using content marketing. Retrieved from http://www.copypress.com/blog/how-to-influence-buyers-using-content-marketing/

[6] Sinkwitz, J. (2016, August 22). Content marketing playbook: Reflections on influencer marketing. Retrieved from https://lseo.com/influencer-marketing/

Or ... because peer discovery[7] is rather inexpensive, you can simply take your last 100 customers and try to match each up with the influencer who appears the most similar in our system, saving more than 200 hours of research time. Buyer persona self-selection in this case works by what on the surface might look like a shotgun approach because it allows you to track which product reviews resulted directly in sales, which not only pads the bottom line, but also actually quickly filters random purchases from lookalike purchasing. The beauty is that the process can be repeated as frequently as you wish to dial in your

buyer personas, and it can help you to test out new audiences without a significant spend.

INFLUENCER MARKETING ISN'T ADVERTISING

Another huge reason to use influencer marketing, and why some suggest that it is likely to be the future of online advertising, is

Photo 2.2. Credit: Sean Stratton

because it isn't subject to the current war on ads via ad blockers and anti-ad blockers. Ad blockers may allow an individual to selectively determine which ad networks and ads a viewer wants to see, but for the most part, they are unable to filter out recommendations and reviews by influencers. Why is that?

According to Nielsen, 84 percent of consumers prefer recommendations from friends and family over other sources of influence—this preference is something that traditional advertising simply cannot reach, despite our collective best efforts by marketers. It's why, while technically possible to filter out FTC-compliant reviews in the future, most likely it will not happen. As a culture, we rely on our friends and family and want to know their experiences, drawing upon crowd-sourced wisdom.

BUILDING BRAND LOYALTY AND THOUGHT LEADERSHIP

By now you understand that consumers finding you through peer influence channels are stickier, less likely to churn, and more likely to become repeat customers. This situation provides not only a brand loyalty opportunity, but also an opportunity to differentiate yourself as a thought leader in your niche. Hearkening back to building out buyer personas, you may have identified several authoritative influencers in the niche that guide your pool of potential consumers for that buyer persona. What would happen if you were to become a peer to those authority figures? By connecting directly with the various authoritative influencers and potential customers alike, you can set yourself up as a thought leader by sharing the information presented by those authorities and getting your information shared by the other authorities—this is authority by proximity. If you are perceived as similar to those individuals whom a potential consumer trusts, then the probability of earning a share of purchases within your niche increases.

INFLUENCER MARKETING PROVIDES FOR PROMOTABLE CONTENT

We'll discuss native advertising and other post-campaign plays later, so for brevity, imagine the following:

1. You engaged an influencer to create a blog product review that was promoted on Twitter. The review, due to Twitter traffic, drove enough in sales to make the campaign worthwhile.

2. The influencer's prominence has actually increased since the initial review and you want to capitalize on that.

3. Some networks make this scenario really easy to take advantage of. With Twitter, you can sponsor someone else's tweet — to their audience or to an entirely new audience. Since the initial tweet and review worked well for sales, you already know that it is ideal for your purposes and good content. Even more, it allows you to test putting out the messaging in front of new audiences and in a way that doesn't look like you're advertising so much as the influencer is advertising. The influencer continues to benefit from the increased exposure, too, so the situation is quite positive.

This example is only one network. Every network has its own nuances, and some ad networks will only like you to use "content" as a landing page for traffic. What better content to use than someone's testimonial for what you're selling?

And if that still isn't enough reason to convince you that influencer marketing needs to be a part of your overall plans ...

YOUR COMPETITORS ARE ALREADY DOING IT

An article by Shane Barker on Social Media Week[8] touched on multiple reasons why you shouldn't be ignoring the concept. The one that should catch your eye is this finding: 60 percent of marketers intended to increase their budget for it this year. Over half of your competition might already be doing this, and in 2017, this figure is almost certainly expected to rise. It's time to get started.

[8] Barker, S. (2016, March 10). 5 reasons why influencer marketing shouldn't be ignored. Retrieved from https://socialmediaweek.org/blog/2016/03/5-reasons-influencer-marketing-shouldnt-ignored/

Photo 3.1. Credit: Andrew Neel.

CHAPTER 3

How to Set Goals for Your Influencer Campaign

Without goals, marketing campaigns are listless and potentially a waste of time and money. Learn the BSQ method (think big, act small, move quickly) as well as the SMART methodology (specific, measurable, actionable, relevant, timeline) to help in the goal-setting process. Next, work through some boosting strategies to get more out of your goals. Plus, get an explanation of how B2B organizations can also partake, dispelling the myth that influencer marketing is for B2C only.

Now that we have discussed what influencer marketing is (Chapter 1) and why it should be a part of your strategy (Chapter 2), Chapter 3 covers how to properly assign the right overall goal to your campaign. Goals or key performance indicators (KPIs) can be determined in a variety of different ways. In this particular chapter, we will cover both the BSQ and SMART methodologies for goal setting, show some simple campaign strategies that match the goal you've chosen, and provide additional thoughts if you're running a B2B campaign.

BSQ IS GOAL SETTING FOR THOSE WHO THINK AGILE

Covered previously[9] by David Van Rooy, the beauty of BSQ is its simplicity:

- B—Think big.
- S—Act small.
- Q—Move quickly.

By setting big, hairy, audacious goals, you won't end up limiting your potential to only what you can conceive of achieving in the near-term future. For instance, as of this writing, we have roughly 30,000 influencing product reviewers[10] in our network. A limited goal might be to reach 100,000 influencers[11]... whereas my ridiculous goal (until it is no longer ridiculous) is to reach a network size of 5 million. The goal is meant to be a major goal vs. something that you can see easily ahead of you.

Acting small in this case simply means taking that goal and dissecting it into achievable milestones. For my own goal that might mean:

1. Write 14 blog posts on how to use influencer marketing — soup to nuts.

2. Create crash course based on the blog posts.

3. Create an e-book based on the course and blog posts.

4. Create a video series to discuss each topic.

5. Hold a series of webinars with CopyPress to cover the video topics.

6. Repeat concept by writing 14 blog posts on how to become a sought-after influencer.

7. Write an article for Forbes, Entrepreneur, Inc, Fortune, The Wall Street Journal, The New York Times, etc.

---

[9] Van Rooy, D. (2015, January 14). BSQ: The only goal-setting framework you will ever need. Retrieved from https://www.inc.com/david-van-rooy/the-only-goal-setting-framework-you-will-ever-need.html

[10] Intellifluence (2016). Find the right influencers and make more sales. Retrieved from https://intellifluence.com/discover?geo=all&network=all&category=all

[11] Intellifluence (2016). Welcome, influencers. Retrieved from https://intellifluence.com/influencers/

8. Get next version featured by Appsumo.

9. Based on traction, get featured (and probably grilled) by jason (Jason Calacanis) on TWIS (thisweekinstartups.com) podcast.

10. Submit 2x version into Product Hunt[12].

None of those tasks is especially improbable. Each simply requires some hard work and harder thinking. As for moving quickly, that's the most obvious of the BSQ methodology—set a deadline for each task and execute it.

How does this apply to goal setting for influencer campaigns? Rather than having a goal of one sale or one review, envision something more grandiose — more than 1,000 directly attributed sales via social from 500 posted reviews across four different social networks. For acting small, it can be based on how you separate outreach with your buyer personas. For instance, if you're selling sports memorabilia like Dennis Goedegebuure of Fanatics, then you likely have those who root for a specific sports team and those who buy for fashion reasons.

Separating your small tasks into the different personas might involve reaching out to 10 New York City fashion-forward bloggers to review Yankees Fitted Hats, and another might be to approach 10 Cubs fans to review their respective fitted hat. In terms of quickness, since you're able to perform 10 outreaches per day without much issue, you could give yourself three days for the initial outreach on these two tasks.

The process flows like a waterfall, with more and more outreach, and more and more transactions as your product reviewers accept the gig and produce for you, eventually reaching your big goal at some point in the future.

NOW LET'S GET SMART

While BSQ is helpful for simply getting moving — with the thesis that any goal is better than no goal (of which I agree) — it is possible to be ... smarter. Initially conceived of by Dave Chaffey's team at Smart Insights[13], the SMART methodology is more nuanced and realistic, which is why I prefer it when determining the "S" portion of my BSQ goal setting:

- **S — SPECIFIC.** The item must be detailed (that is, 1,000 new brand signups[14] vs. more brand signups).

- **M — MEASURABLE.** Fuzzy goals need not apply; we have to be able to actually measure and track the goal

[12] Sinkwitz, J. (2016, August 29). Optimizing for Product Hunt: How not to. Retrieved from https://theascent.biz/optimizing-for-product-hunt-how-not-to-74ed01a4e7a9

[13] Chaffey, D. (2017, April 6). How to define SMART marketing objectives. Retrieved from http://www.smartinsights.com/goal-setting-evaluation/goals-kpis/define-smart-marketing-objectives/

[14] Intellifluence (2016). Hello, brands. Retrieved from https://intellifluence.com/brands

Photo 3.2. Credit: David Marcu

- **A—ACTIONABLE.** Within the context of Intellifluence, since there's actions associated, you're covered. (Note: In some versions of SMART, the "A" stands for attainable.)

- **R — RELEVANT.** Is the goal aligned with your need as a marketer? Sales, visibility, reach ... yes.

- **T — TIMELINE.** Similar to BSQ using deadlines, there needs to be a time-based component.

In my opinion, the biggest difference between BSQ and SMART is that BSQ gets you moving and SMART helps you focus on moving more in the right direction. Theoretically, you could assign the wrong big-thinking goal, whereas within the SMART methodology, that's less likely to happen since you're applying critical thinking to whether or not the goal is actionable and relevant. In later iterations of the concept, SMARTER has emerged, with ER representing Evaluate and Re-evaluate. I would agree with this report as a post-mortem procedure on any marketing campaign, but for our purposes, my KPI on this article is getting you to at least use goals when diving into influencer marketing.

SIMPLE CAMPAIGN BOOSTING STRATEGIES TO GET MORE OUT OF YOUR GOALS

You have some goals. You have a rough plan. Let's maximize those efforts with a few sample strategies:

1. BE GENEROUS.

On our platform, a business and an influencer can negotiate on what activity will be performed and for what type of compensation. However, by going over the top, you can almost ensure that the review you receive is going to result in an equally over-the-top attention (most of the time). For instance, if you are the Fanatics sending out the Cubs cap, what if you also threw in some additional Cubs swag? If the persona is a Cubs fan, that addition is going to be highly appreciated.

2. REUSE CONTENT.

The product reviewers created some great visual content and wrote some beautiful words about your product. Now what? Aggregate the positive feedback and feature it in an infographic hosted on your own site, sharing back to the very same influencers with whom you worked. In many cases, as humans, we're inclined to respond to ego bait, and you'll get some shares from those looking to highlight their own work. This technique also works as a piece that can be circulated to your prospect email list (if you don't have one, you need to build one).

3. USE SECONDARY INFLUENCERS FOR AMPLIFICATION.

Let's say in your first round of reviews you ended up with several great blog posts, some tweets, and other recognition. You were smart and also managed to reuse the content for some hosted material for your own site. One simple way to get a lot more out of those reviews would then be to approach those influencers who fit tangentially into your campaign and ask them to promote what was already created. I love these tactics because it allows you to get the most out of created content. While this group of influencers might not be exactly what you want for direct reviews, if the demographics overlap enough, then the spread will result in more of your buyer personas being exposed to the messaging.

WHAT ABOUT B2B

Marketers who focus on B2B products and services often find themselves frustrated at seeing all the incredible things that can be done with traditional B2C campaigns. But they are usually faced with longer sales cycles, sophisticated buyers, and deal with — for lack of a better word — increased complexity.

Typically, we see four rough types of B2B marketing goals:

1. Engagement

2. Mindshare and thought leadership

3. Customer acquisition (direct sale)

4. Lead gen (sales funnel entry)

B2B marketers will be most familiar with SMART methodologies discussed earlier, so these four goal types get folded into the process. On the "how," within Intellifluence specifically, that area isn't fairly easy to explain. Both customer acquisition and lead gen fall into the direct buyer persona approach with the goal of achieving an action.

If the sale can be handled as part of a multi-step form, then it is possible to acquire the minimally required fields like email and name to push into a drip email campaign for lead

nurturing. Otherwise, if the remaining fields are completed, a sale is achieved.
For mindshare and engagement, the goal here is more on audience size than specificity.
Although not mutually exclusive—harkening back to authoritative influence — it is
still necessary to be relevant in order to achieve mindshare, with not all engagement
being equal.

Ask any auto dealership, and those in charge will tell you the huge time suck between
car buyers and tire kickers who lack a budget (but ones who are simply in love with the
process). Engaging time wasters is a good way to waste time that could be spent closing
real prospects.

Photo 4.1. Credit: Jan Vašek.

CHAPTER 4

Who Exactly Are You Trying to Influence?

Explore the four factors governing consumer behavior (cultural, social, personal, and psychological) as well as their respective components (geographic, language, historical, religious culture, and cultural environmental), (family, socioeconomic status, and social groups), (age, lifestyle, and personality), and (motivation, perception, learning, beliefs and attitudes). Using Up Hail as a case study, the four factors and their component considerations are used to create a buyer persona that could be used as the target buyer and user in an influencer marketing campaign.

In the previous chapter we discussed how to set influencer campaign goals. It is time to get more nuanced for Chapter 4 and delve into the underlying psychology and factors surrounding who you are trying to influence when building out buyer personas as a brand[15]. To make this effort, let's explore the four factors that influence consumer behavior.

THE FOUR FACTORS INFLUENCING CONSUMER BEHAVIOR

Covered in great detail by Fanny Perreau of The Consumer Factor, the four factors we're chiefly concerned with are:

CULTURAL FACTORS
Geographic, language, historical, religious culture, and cultural environmental

SOCIAL FACTORS
Family, socioeconomic status, and social groups (education, sports, etc.)

PERSONAL FACTORS
Age, lifestyle, and personality

PSYCHOLOGICAL FACTORS
Motivation, perception, learning, beliefs, and attitudes

When we briefly covered how to determine buyer personas (see Chapter 2), it was entirely based upon mining existing customer data to infer future prospective customers. Let's spend some time trying to understand how that methodology would need to be tweaked in order to satisfy the four primary factors that influence consumer behavior.

As an example for this thought exercise, let's use my friend Avi A. Wilensky and his ride-sharing app Up Hail. For those who haven't used it yet, Up Hail takes the guesswork out of whether people should use a service like Uber, Lyft, or any of the other dozens of services out there. It works by simultaneously querying based on your origin and destination inputs to figure out where you'll get the most inexpensive ride — simple, useful, on my phone.

Now, let's say Avi has pulled together a lot of data from his current customer base and has been defining personas. How might these personas change based on the following factors?

CULTURAL FACTORS FOR UP HAIL

1. **GEOGRAPHY.** I would imagine that this item is going to be one of the biggest factors, culturally, that impacts the buyer persona. There's a strong correlation between urban population centers and usage of ride-sharing apps, so one tweak that could be made in addition to pulling previous customer data would be to skew toward ZIP codes that have high populations. Thanks to the U.S. Census, this data

---

[15] Intellifluence (2016). Hello brands, Retrieved from https://intellifluence.com/brands

is available[16] for consumption and could be used to drive peer influence or even general social ad campaigns.

2. **LANGUAGE.** I have only ever used the app in English, but there are many languages spoken throughout the world, and it is exceptionally difficult to try and accommodate them all. Therefore, language becomes a good filtering tool. While it may seem harsh, you should filter out those whom you can't readily support in order to ensure the peers on your buyer persona match as closely as possible AND are those you can impact in a positive way.

3. **HISTORICAL & RELIGIOUS.** For the most part, there is likely to be little impact, culturally from those of certain religious or societally historical backgrounds. The only exceptions I can think of are certain groups (Amish as an obvious example) that would be opposed to using such a service, but they are generally inaccessible online. Religion, to a degree, could be a factor for those where a female driver cannot be present, but that is a weaker filter in my opinion, and it probably can be paired with geography in the future to create a new accommodating feature.

Photo 4.2. Credit: Anubhav Saxena

SOCIAL FACTORS FOR UP HAIL

1. **SOCIOECONOMIC.** By and large, this factor should be the most significant factor. Who can afford a smartphone? Nowadays, this area is less an issue, but as recently as five years ago, it would have been a significant filtering method. Where the factor would come into play more is in the differences between iOS and Android, where, for the most part, iOS users tend to be wealthier and thus have a higher degree of disposable income. This gap has since closed over the years, but it still is an opportunity when targeting on a device usage level (data an app is likely

[16] United States Census Bureau (2017). American Fact Finder: Community facts. Retrieved from https://factfinder.census.gov/faces/nav/jsf/pages/index.xhtml

to have). Who can afford to use ride sharing or taxis? This issue is the bigger issue, but, again, potentially solved by focusing on the device used to access the app. Additionally, this filter could be paired up for those urban density areas lacking a reliable, or rather desired, mode of public transportation. When in San Francisco, I personally would much rather use Up Hail than the BART, as a personal preference. In Munich or London, I don't mind the bahn and tube as much.

2. **FAMILY.** We could quote the movie "Inception" here because familial influence is influence within influence. While parental figures can help guide and direct purchasing decisions, the reverse is also true. My in-laws were casual Uber users until I had them install Up Hail on their phones. Now, they use whatever service is the cheapest. The familial tie is greater in some products than others (Coke vs. Pepsi families, for instance), but for Up Hail, I do not think it is a significant factor.

3. **SOCIAL GROUPS.** This filter could be a decent filter, especially since it dovetails so nicely into true peer influence[17] groups. Not all social groups are created equal, so it is important to apply critical thinking. Let's say that I'm a University of Arizona Basketball fan (I am). Let's say I also go to some games and might consume beverages before or during the game, using Up Hail afterward to responsibly and safely get home—those in my peer group who also are a fan of college basketball and alcoholic beverages would make for an excellent filter, as the need for the product is high. I'm also in groups related to artificial intelligence, but the correlations would be much weaker, except for possibly understanding technology and thus being willing to test out a mobile app.

PERSONAL FACTORS FOR UP HAIL

1. **AGE.** Age initially would have been a good indicator for mobile app usage, but the line has blurred considerably. So long as a person is older than 18, the individual is a worthwhile persona to target. Granted, Generation X might be ideal due to socioeconomic reasons of having more disposable income and prolonged exposure to technology, but baby boomer usage of mobile apps has climbed significantly over the years.

2. **PERSONALITY.** Introverted or extroverted probably isn't a major factor on app usage, although possibly those on the agoraphobic scale would have slightly higher usage metrics due to fears of mass transit and crowds.

3. **LIFESTYLE.** This area is the big variable within personal factors. Sedentary vs. active is a key for short-distance fares where some will choose to bike or walk and some will prefer to get a ride. The same goes toward lifestyle choices surrounding

[17] Evans, A. (2016, September 15). The power of the peer influencer. Retrieved from https://blog.intellifluence.com/the-power-of-the-peer-influencer-6c7eaadbfa85

saving or spending. Active spenders are far more likely to spend a few dollars taking an Uber than those who count every penny.

Photo 4.3 Credit: Luke Porter

PSYCHOLOGICAL FACTORS FOR UP HAIL

1. **MOTIVATION.** This item ties back into the peer influence concepts discussed in our first chapter and why peer influence is so important. What is the subconscious need for Up Hail? One simple measure that I can think of is the need to save money, a scarcity factor. Once peer influencers[13] are identified, the impact of a fast query that saves money vs. blindly using any one ride-sharing app is ample motivation. Other motivating factors would include speed, of which executive employment might satisfy. Where time is money, the app is useful.

2. **PERCEPTION.** This one is difficult to access via customer data. What would be required is some sort of survey to get a better understanding as to how an initial advertisement or recommendation was perceived. One possible way to use this area on developing buyer personas, though, would be to determine if multiple viewings of an ad were required in order to convert. In other words, if targeting pixels are used, and it appears as though a consumer needed more than three exposures to Up Hail before converting to an app download, then the consumer might be slightly ad blind to the brand. This item is less of a persona filter than an overall brand image tweak, though.

3. **LEARNING.** Usage of the app at higher levels would imply learning and acceptance. This area could be used when filtering out buyer personas by subsegmenting the group for those who appear to be the most likely to turn into

brand evangelists, of which those can be used later on for content marketing purposes.

4. **BELIEFS AND ATTITUDES.** This data might be culled by tying app reviews to app usage. When positive experiences are noted, look for similarities among the positive reviewers to determine if any subsections of buyer personas exist. The beliefs that are the most helpful are those where the app is viewed as necessary and important, and they are going to also be the mostly likely to positively review in other platforms for free or for some compensation related to their next ride.

HOW TO USE THESE BUYER PERSONALS IN INTELLIFLUENCE

Between the initial chapter on data gathering for buyer personas, and this chapter on how to dissect them into various consumer factors, let's assume that you have some incredible buyer personas. The next step is to pitch influencers who best match the peers of those buyer personas and attempt to maximize your social sales. In all likelihood, from building out the personas, you have a keen understanding of which channels are going to be the most appropriate for your audience. If not, we'll discuss that area deeper in our next chapter.

Photo 5.1. Credit: fancycrave1

CHAPTER 5

Which Social Channel Will Bring Sales for Your Business?

Which social channel is the best fit for your campaign? Explore using a usefulness matrix that examines the merits based on open reach, visual nature, casual acceptance, professional acceptance, and capacity for details. Using case studies from Antavo, Hubspot, Tinder, and Fanatics, see how the channel selection differs based on product type and B2B vs. B2C focus.

Welcome to Chapter 5. So far we have discussed:

1. What is influencer marketing? (Chapter 1)

2. Why should it be a part of your strategy? (Chapter 2)

3. How can you set campaign goals for it? (Chapter 3)

4. Whom should you try to influence? (Chapter 4)

The next logical step in the process is to discuss channel selection and provide some case studies as examples. Knowing who you're targeting and what your goals are, it is now important to understand where to focus, based on your specific needs. Not all social channels are created equal and not all will be effective for all types of businesses, so let's dive in.

INTELLIFLUENCE SOCIAL CHANNEL USEFULNESS MATRIX

The following channels are currently available for matching influencers[19] and brands[20] at Intellifluence. For the purposes of this chapter, we excluded Amazon[21] since it is a special case. This listing is not meant to be a comprehensive list of every social network's usefulness, largely because it becomes a slippery slope of inclusion and what might be a 2,000-word chapter would become 20,000 trying to include all the various clones and limited audience networks that exist.

NETWORK	Open Reach	Visual	Casual	Professional	Detailed
Blog	Y	Y	Y	Y	Y
Facebook	N	Y	Y	Y	Y
Instagram	Y	Y	Y	N	N
LinkedIn	N	N	N	Y	Y
Pinterest	Y	Y	Y	N	N
Twitter	Y	Y	Y	Y	N
YouTube	Y	Y	Y	Y	Y

Graphic 5.1. Influencer channels. Source: Intellifluence

For simple definitions, the columns represent a surface "yes" or "no" on the following questions:

1. **OPEN REACH.** Is the reach of the post open for most anyone to view it? In the case of blogs, tweets, pins, and YouTube videos, that answer is usually a "yes." It is possible to have private channels, but they are rarer. Instagram does have a higher incidence of private accounts than Pinterest, but the majority are still open. Facebook and LinkedIn are the notable exclusions. Fan pages on Facebook

[19] Intellifluence (2016). Welcome, influencers. Retrieved from https://intellifluence.com/influencers/

[20] Intellifluence (2016). Hello, brands. Retrieved from https://intellifluence.com/brands

[21] Sinkwitz, J. (2016, October 3). Amazon: No more incentivized reviews". Retrieved from https://blog.intellifluence.com/amazon-no-more-incentivized-reviews-d109ad66ad64

are open, but most Facebook posts are set to the "friends" setting, which limits the audience exposure. Similarly, unless you are explicitly following or otherwise connected to an individual on LinkedIn, you won't see the posts.

2. **VISUAL.** Is the network capable of supporting visual content? More than just technical capable, which all are, does the audience accept and request visual content? In the past couple of years, Twitter moved into the "yes" category, with the lone holdout being LinkedIn. It is possible to share visual content on LinkedIn, but it generally does not fit with expectations. Most LinkedIn users complain of the Facebookification of the connection feed with non-business posts.

3. **CASUAL.** Is it acceptable to post casual information? Blogs are a somewhat special case since each publication is sure to be different in editorial policy, but, presumably, so long as an influencer is interested in reviewing a product, a casual tone would not be an issue. Once again, the holdout is LinkedIn, where a casual tone runs counter to professional decorum.

4. **PROFESSIONAL.** Finally, a signal that strongly benefits LinkedIn. Technically, professional tone may not be accepted on certain blog channels as the inverse of the casual discussion in the previous post, and some Twitter and Facebook channels might not be the right place for an appropriate discussion, but that item is tone specific. For the most part, the only two channels in our experience that tend to not skew professional are Instagram and Pinterest, which has more to do with the extreme visual nature of the platforms than anything else.

5. **DETAILED.** Is it possible to provide a comprehensive review of a product or service? Yes, it is possible to provide a brief blurb of a blog post and link to it from Twitter or from a Pinterest pin. But for the purposes of self-contained posts, this feature is meant to be used as a filter when a lot of information needs to be conveyed in a single setting.

Let's put this selection into practice with some mini case studies on campaign building that you can use as examples after you get started using influencer marketing and want to start selling more over social.

B2B ENTERPRISE BUYERS

- Created for: Timi Garai
- Company: Antavo

Before we can determine which channels to target, it is important to build a buyer persona. As a quick and dirty way of doing this tactic, I pulled up the Antavo Loyalty Twitter account and started dissecting its followers. Note that Antavo bills itself as loyalty marketing software for e-commerce companies to build reward programs, so I decided to find followers that fit the criteria. Interestingly, while I fully expected to find a plethora of e-com companies, what I found more interesting is the number of e-com consultants. Perfect.

SAMPLE BUYER PERSONA:

- Title: Owner and analyst
- Industry: e-commerce, consulting
- College-educated
- Age and gender neutral
- Influenced by data

What could Antavo do with this data? Could it build a campaign that works? Its product is complex, with a long sales process, and it caters to professionals.

STEP 1: Find those peers

Thankfully, this item is going to be very easy for Antavo. Pulling up LinkedIn Sales Navigator, I plugged in some e-com and analyst filters to see that, with some effort, more than 20,000 individuals could be targeted.

STEP 2: What do these peers want?

Prestige and value. One significant value add that I can see for this process would be to

Graphic 5.2. Source: Intellifluence

build out a multi-channel campaign that plays to the egos of the buyer persona and then use that campaign to attract more peers.

STEP 3: Channels that work

For the purposes of this sample, I would use blogs, LinkedIn, and Twitter in the following way...

1. Outreach to provide a discount on the Antavo service for those who sign up via the chosen sample reviewer (e-com consultant) in exchange for a comprehensive blog post on the reviewer's blog.

2. Reviewer shares blog post on LinkedIn.

3. Reviewer then tweets a link to the review post.

4. Antavo conducts an interview with the review for the Antavo blog.

5. Process repeats for 10 reviewers.

6. Antavo takes the 10 interviews generated and creates an e-book download on "10 out of 10 e-com consultants can't be wrong," which is made available for the price of an email address.

7. Antavo re-engages the 10 reviewers to share the e-book on LinkedIn, Twitter, and their personal blogs.

8. Antavo taps into the Twitter ad platform to target lookalike audiences of reviewer lists (or to the LinkedIn Sales Navigator broader email list).

9. Antavo sales team aggressively targets the rest of the list via LinkedIn, sending the e-book out for social proof.

Such campaigns are not easy, but having spent the majority of my career in digital B2B, I can attest to the process yielding dividends.

B2B SMALLER/MID-SIZED BUSINESS

- Created for: Matthew Barby
- Company: HubSpot

HubSpot makes for an interesting case because the company has so many different products all throughout the small- and medium-sized business market. In some ways, this arrangement makes life more difficult

Graphic 5.3. Source. LinkedIn Groups

because one needs to focus on a specific buyer persona when building out the campaign idea. Looking at the HubSpot Twitter account, it is too noisy—some are fans, some are following to learn, some are industry players. It is still doable, but to show another way to do this step, we can look into area user groups on LinkedIn.

Peeking behind the group curtain, we find a large number of "inbound marketing" titles, many of which are mid-career (manager through director). But once again, the prevalent buyer persona being built by sorting through the list is not that of end users, but instead of consultants. If we were to go through this channel, the channel selection would end up being similar to that of Antavo, so we're going to pick a secondary buyer persona, one of end users for the inbound sales platform.

SAMPLE BUYER PERSONA:

- Title: E-commerce manager
- Industry: Open
- Company size: 11–50

- Negatives: HubSpot

STEP 1: Find those peers

According to LinkedIn Sales Navigator, this listing is an even more impressive list, and one I currently have saved for future sales purposes. Nearly 66,000 individuals who don't mention HubSpot are possible buyers.

STEP 2: What do the peers want?

While prestige and ego bait are nearly universal in practice, to provide an alternative angle of approach, we can take the strict review path and offer an incentive by providing compensated Pro accounts.

STEP 3: Channels that work

Similar to B2B Enterprise, we are looking at blog, LinkedIn, and Twitter as the primary channels. For a wrinkle, I'll throw in YouTube.

1. Outreach to a large number of the e-commerce managers (about 100) to provide compensated Pro accounts, with the option at the end of a 30-day evaluation period to write a blog post on the site in which the Pro account is used OR to do a recorded Hangout or Skype interview to be posted on the e-com site's YouTube channel.

2. Reviewer shares blog post or video link on LinkedIn.

3. Reviewer tweets link to the review URL.

4. HubSpot systematically shares a highlighted review and day on its LinkedIn account.

5. HubSpot sources video reviews with an intro on its YouTube channel.

6. HubSpot amplifies all tweets to reviewer audience and look-alike audience.

7. HubSpot amplifies LinkedIn shares to its Showcase page through sponsored content ads.

8. Reviews are added to a drip campaign on existing flow for HubSpot trial accounts.

9. State of e-commerce sales white paper gets created by HubSpot, aggregating data from the approximately 100 users to show how quickly results can be had for using its sales platform.

10. The white paper is used to provide a top-of-funnel approach for a secondary drip campaign.

The difficulty in building out a campaign for HubSpot is the company already eats and breathes this type of campaign. Given that it has such a large organization and can focus, I think it'd be interesting to see how effective it would be to run such a campaign on a continual basis, choosing 100 e-com managers per month, resulting in a constant influx of links, honest reviews, and video assets which would be difficult for competitors to match in intensity.

B2C MOBILE APPS

- Created for: Brian Norgard
- Company: Tinder

How can I do this case study without getting in trouble? For those of you not familiar with Tinder, the year is 2016, and it is a heavily used casual dating app. What makes it an intriguing case study is that it is not often something one expects to see throughout social feeds. There are quite a few buyer personas one could create based on the data Brian likely has on usage, but for simplicity, we'll focus on areas where social proof is the most effective.

SAMPLE BUYER PERSONA:

- Gender: Male
- Age: 18–30
- Other: not currently a tinder boost user

Step 1: Find those peers

Since we're no longer dealing with a professional focus, we can leave LinkedIn out of the equation. For fun, we can use Instagram and look for snipe competitors at the same time by pulling followers of accounts like eHarmony.

Step 2: What do the peers want?

Do I have to really answer this question? The peers want butterflies, rainbows, and sunshine — also a date. In order to satisfy the primary demand, a month of "Boost" for free would elicit the expected response.

Step 3: Channels that work

For our purposes, let's stick with Instagram. I can conceive of how to make this network work on Twitter and Facebook as well, but I think a visual story will say everything necessary.

1. Outreach, sorting descending by follower count, to the male followers of the eHarmony account (and others—this is only a quick example). In exchange, a user needs to post a screenshot (anonymizing who is matched, of course) with how quickly he received a positive response to a date.

2. The reviewer posts the screenshot on Instagram noting that he used Tinder Boost and had plans for the evening in X minutes.

Believe it or not, this list is probably sufficient. As discussed in previous posts, the peer influence among other males ages 18 to 30 who see how quickly a potentially lonely evening was turned into a date is quite strong. The point is not so much to engage and interact on behalf of Tinder, but to allow the outcome of the product to speak for itself.

B2C FASHION

- Created for: Dennis Goedegebuure
- Company: Fanatics

We've spoken about Fanatics before in another chapter, referencing Yankees and Cubs, but this maker of all entertainment apparel could use with one more case study. The company does have different buyer personas that skew toward either fashion choices or fan choices, but in this case, it is time for something special.

Step 1: Find those peers

Photo 5.2. Credit: University of Arizona

There are numerous ways to find this peer group, but one easy way would be to consume the Twitter hashtag usage looking for super fans. Another great method would be to hunt on Facebook Groups for [college + sport] combinations and interacting with the various communities found therein.

Step 2: What do the peers want?

Swag. Respect. Prestige.

Step 3: Channels that work

Using humor for this campaign, let's pick YouTube, Facebook, Twitter, and Instagram.

1. Outreach occurs to a certain overweight guy in Arizona that loves UofA basketball.

2. The reviewer is sent a jersey.

3. The reviewer films a compilation video of various people dunking on him mercilessly, preferably using former UofA stars for additional celebrity influence.

4. The review gets posted natively to each platform and edited down for Instagram stories.

5. Sports stars involved in the humor get appropriately tagged.

6. Celebrities will most likely share on their own volition. Fanatics can share on its channels, continuing on with its impressive super fan series. On each share, tie-in

buttons created to purchase specific apparel get used directly from the Fanatics store.

TAKEAWAY

No matter whether B2B or B2C, it is possible to include influence as part of the overall campaign and have it work. The biggest consideration needs to be consistency of channel usage that best fits the constraints of the chosen buyer persona.

Photo 6.1. Credit: Ed Gregory

CHAPTER 6

Determining the Right Influencer Type for Your Campaign

Referencing the earlier chapters, learn which of the three influencer types (aspirational, authoritative, and peer) would work best for you by using another usefulness matrix. To explain the proper times to use each influencer type, walk through case studies generated for Murray Newlands, Slack, and Search Engine Journal.

You've set goals[22] for your influencer marketing campaign; you have an idea of who you are looking to target[23]. In Chapter 6, it is time to break down the major influencer types to help you understand when to employ each within your overall marketing strategy.

THREE TYPES OF INFLUENCERS

If you look back in the first chapter[24] of the series, you'll recall that at Intellifluence we like to segment influencers into three main categories: aspirational, authoritative, and peer[25]. The reason is fairly simple: Each category is best used for specific types of campaigns. While some overlap can occur, for the vast majority of brands[26] looking

Photo 6.2. Credit: matrix.wikia.com

to deploy an influence campaign, the goals and reach mechanisms required to meet those goals for the specific buyer personas tend to fall within one of the chosen categories.

So when should you use a celebrity (aspirational) campaign? What about authority? Peer? Similar to our breakdown on when to use specific social channels[27], the best way forward is with a Matrix.

INTELLIFLUENCE INFLUENCER TYPE USEFULNESS MATRIX

Not going to lie ... I love categorizing data into tables in order to help make better sense of the world around me. Hopefully, if it works for me, it'll also work for you. Rather than a "Y" or "N" like we used on the social channel table to describe binary answers, the influencer types are more fluid. Thus, we use a 1, 2, or 3 (with 3 being the highest score) to explain the power a type possesses for each attribute.

TYPE	Reach	Relevancy	Trust	Inform	Commerce	Emotion
Aspirational	3	1	1	1	1	2
Authoritative	2	2	2	3	2	1
Peer	1	3	3	2	3	3

Graphic 6.1. Source: Intellifluence

For our purposes, the first three (reach, relevancy, and trust) are the most important attributes. Capability of informing, directing commerce, and eliciting an emotional response

---

[22] Sinkwitz, J. (2016, September 28). How to set goals for your influencer campaign. Retrieved from https://blog.intellifluence.com/how-to-set-goals-for-your-influencer-campaign-abc236257f79

[23] Sinkwitz, J. (2016, October 5). Who exactly are you trying to influence? Retrieved from https://blog.intellifluence.com/who-are-you-trying-to-influence-ba8ddaf5a575

[24] Sinkwitz, J. (2016, September 13). What is influencer marketing? Retrieved from https://blog.intellifluence.com/what-is-influencer-marketing-40549fe706b4

[25] Evans, A. (2016, September 15). The power of the peer influencer. Retrieved from https://blog.intellifluence.com/the-power-of-the-peer-influencer-6c7eaadbfa85

[26] Intellifluence (2016). Hello, brands. Retrieved from https://intellifluence.com/brands

[27] Sinkwitz, J. (2016, October 11). Which social channel will bring sales for your business? Retrieved from https://blog.intellifluence.com/which-social-channel-will-bring-sales-for-your-business-c8831fb0c4e2

are secondary factors that exist primarily because of the first three, rather than by itself.

Let's explain why in the definition of each:

1. Reach. The simplest to define, reach is simply primary and secondary audience size. Naturally, celebrities will have the largest overall audience size, and their words will tend to be carried the most.

2. Relevancy. While not an inverse to reach, it is often the case that similarities examined in a buyer persona result in an overall smaller set of potential people simply due to being more targeted. How relevant am I to do online marketing? Very: It is what I have been doing longer than anything else professionally in my life (eating doesn't count). Shoe selection? Not at all. I can't even find a pair of men's size 13 shoes that fit right, so you can safely ignore any suggestions I give you.

3. Trust. We trust our friends, family, and peers significantly more than we trust the random celebrity .... If you don't, you really should, because they are right far more often than the random celebrity you might aspire toward.

4. Inform. The capacity to inform is a combination of relevancy and core knowledge, backed by trust. Peers provide a decent degree of educational aptitude, but this area is where authoritative influences thrive. Are you more likely to share the political Facebook post of your friend and family member or the person posting on an "authoritative" publication? Sorry, Uncle Bob.

5. Commerce. The root of all commerce is the confluence of trust and need. According to our matrix, we can see that since peers lead the influencer types for each of these categories, it possesses the highest capacity to influence a commercial decision, adjusted on a per person basis of course, because audience size becomes a factor as a multiplier when attempting to calculate potential sales volume.

6. Emotion. Eliciting an emotional response is a tricky factor. While partly based on relevancy (and thus empathetic connection), it is also based somewhat paradoxically on reach—the more people that share a specific response, the more likely the herd mentality kicks in.

So which is best? Each type can be used for different goals, but if you were to assume that each value is equivalent and simply add up the scores:

TYPE	SCORE
Aspirational	9
Authoritative	12
Peer	13

Graphic 6.2. Source: Intellifluence

I bet that makes you want to get out and discover some peers[28] right away. You can wait,

---

[28] Intellifluence (2016). Find the right influencers and make more sales. Retrieved from https://intellifluence.com/discover?geo=all&networ k=all&category=all

though, because to be fair to each type, I developed some quick case studies on how each main influencer type could be properly utilized.

USING ASPIRATIONAL INFLUENCE

Do you know Murray Newlands? If you're on Vine or Twitter, there's a decent chance that you do. This marketer and entrepreneur turned major influencer is everywhere these days. So why would someone that is already an authoritative influencer via his Entrepreneur and Forbes columns use aspirational influence?

Photo 6 3 Credit: Twitter

Math.

Yes, that is Murray with the immortal Tyra Banks. When it comes to gaining overall influence to transition from an authority to a celebrity (*remember, some authorities can transcend to celebrity status), the most important element is audience size. Thus, by proximity and co-occurrence campaigns of Murray posing for pictures and doing joint events with other celebrities, his ability to radically increase his follower counts happens due to 2+2 equaling 5.

Fame builds fame.

In my opinion, if Murray wants to keep building up his name, he's going about it the right way. Next, I would recommend that he backfill using peer influencers to reinforce his authoritative status by increase share counts and other CPA activity tied to his professional postings, offering reciprocal co-occurrence selfies at the numerous conferences he attends.

USING AUTHORITATIVE INFLUENCE

At Intellifluence, we use Slack for the vast majority of our communications. Zendesk tickets go into our support channel. Stripe transactions and registration events have their own channel. Our product roadmap sits in a channel of its own and feeds into sprints on Asana. Git commits go in the dev channel, etc. I'm a convert.

How did I become a convert though? It wasn't necessarily a peer, even though Dave Snyder first introduced me to it at CopyPress—rather it was from reading this article[29] by Scott Rosenberg and giving it another try and seeing the power of a hub that lived up to its hype.

How can Slack make more use out of authoritative influencers?

Frankly, they're doing a great job. If you're reading any tech or startup journalist for a long enough time, chances are you'll see them write an article on Slack. However, that is also where I think they should continue focusing.

---

[29] Rosenberg, S. (2015, May 8). Shut down your office. You now work in Slack. Retrieved from https://www.wired.com/2015/05/shut-down-your-office-you-now-work-in-slack/

By ensuring a blanket PR campaign of simply announcing new integrations jointly with their partners and gaining coverage, they'll continue in their never-ending campaign to optimize the way we consume information and make sense of it at the business level.

Next, they can use peer influencers to amplify the effects of these positive PR pushes by offering discounted "Standard" plans for those with existing Slack plans that are willing to share out and review their positive experiences. That kind of authoritative plus peer influence helps to create a purchasing compulsion for anyone obsessed with productivity.

USING PEER INFLUENCE

You didn't think that a peer influencer marketplace was going to end the article there, did you?

For our final case, we turn to our friends at Search Engine Journal, founded by Loren Baker and under the watchful editorial eye of Kelsey Jones.

SEJ is in an interesting position since it is one of only a handful of search news sites, which largely share authors and cover the same set of events and strategies In itself, it would be classified as an authoritative influencer. I won't pretend to speak for it, but as a goal, let's say they want to increase advertising. That goal is accomplished by both increasing readership and increasing demand for ad space.

How can peers help?

The more shares and eyeballs each article gets, the more attractive it becomes to advertisers. SEJ could do that today by using a variety of search and social tools, and making use of influencer marketing to constantly push for more readership, but it can go further than that. By offering high-level peers an opportunity to post their own 10x content (no lightweight guest posts — this is a serious journal after all) in its outreach in exchange for a speaking slot at SEJ Summit, consulting leadflow, or some other ego-stroking item of value, they can continue their stride toward editorial excellence and convince those authoritative in the industry that don't write much to share their knowledge a bit more freely, and only with SEJ. This approach creates a differentiation from among its own peers, and thus increases niche advertising demand that matches the audience shift away from the commoditization of search journalism.

As you can see from the case studies and usefulness matrix, all types of influence have their place. It is just a matter of ensuring that the type you need best fits into your overall marketing strategy[30].

[30] Sinkwitz, J. (2016, September 19) Why should influencer marketing be a part of your strategy? Retrieved from https://blog.intellifluence.com/why-should-influencer-marketing-be-a-part-of-your-strategy-88122ece9dab

Photo 7.1. Credit: Blake Bronstad

CHAPTER 7

Time to Pick the Right Product Influencers

Learn how to calculate which product influencer is best suited for your campaign based on the simple equation of Outcome = (Reach * Engagement * Relevance) — Cost. Using Joe S vs. Damien T as influencers, see how the decision to use one over the other differs based on the variable inputs for different situations. The primary reason for this calculation is to dispel the myth of audience size being everything when considering which influencers to work with.

This is Chapter 7. You're just about halfway done—believe me when I say that if you read from the beginning[31] to the end, you'll be more versed on influencer marketing than 90 percent of the industry that actively sells the service for a living. In this segment, we're going to focus on selecting the right product influencers[32]. In order for this to make sense we're going to need to assume four things:

1. You have a defined goal for campaign success[33].

2. You have a strong understanding of who your intended buyer is[34].

3. You know which social channels[35] you want to target.

4. You understand the type of influencer[36] you are targeting.

PROBABILITY OF INFLUENCE

I know what you're thinking.

It's OK. I'm not a mathematician, and during my MBA program, I often left early in my statistics class, so we'll not develop true probabilistic models. Instead, let's treat this approach like some simple algebra.

Outcome = (Reach * Engagement * Relevance)—Cost

It was my understanding there would be no math.

Photo 7.2. Credit: HaveToWinToPlay (Reddit)

Yes, this equation is overly simplified, but really not by much. Let's discuss.

REACH

Reach in this definition is just the primary reach. There are ways to measure secondary reach based on how many people are seeing a message when it is shared, retweeted, or re-pinned, but for the sake of our simple calculations, we're using audience size as a measurement of reach, and, of course, that audience size is based on a single social channel. Otherwise, comparing someone's Instagram reach to someone else's YouTube reach would

---

[31] Sinkwitz, J. (2016, September 13). What is influencer marketing? Retrieved from https://blog.intellifluence.com/what-is-influencer-marketing-40549fe706b4

[32] Intellifluence (2016). Welcome, influencers. Retrieved from https://intellifluence.com/influencers/

[33] Sinkwitz, J. (2016, September 28). How to set goals for your influencer campaign. Retrieved from https://blog.intellifluence.com/how-to-set-goals-for-your-influencer-campaign-abc236257f79

[34] Sinkwitz, J. (2016, October 5). Who exactly are you trying to influence? Retrieved from https://blog.intellifluence.com/who-are-you-trying-to-influence-ba8ddaf5a575

[35] Sinkwitz, J. (2016, October 11). Which social channel will bring sales for your business? Retrieved from https://blog.intellifluence.com/which-social-channel-will-bring-sales-for-your-business-c8831fb0c4e2

[36] Sinkwitz, J. (2016, October 18). Determining the right influencer type for your campaign. Retrieved from https://blog.intellifluence.com/determining-the-right-influencer-type-for-your-campaign-837a8fe94ff2

be to enter the apples and oranges conundrum. Raw audience size as a number can be used here.

ENGAGEMENT

Engagement is a measurement to show what percentage of posts receive some degree of liking, sharing, or comments, etc. The reason it is important is because it is possible to find an influencer with an extremely large audience of followers that have largely tuned out, effectively ad blind. Also, it helps to identify which audiences are fake—it isn't hard nor expensive to buy 100,000 Twitter followers. It is, however, more expensive to buy 100,000 Twitter followers and purchase daily engagement from all of them. Since there can be varying degrees of engagement, for simplicity reasons, we are going to use engagement as a percentage, looking at a random sampling of posts and seeing how many of those posts had any engagement. For your own calculations you could choose to assign different values for different levels of engagement, though we find this tactic is a rough filter that effectively provides the same answer with less calculation.

RELEVANCE

Similar to engagement, this item is also a percentage and is going to be different for every single product and channel combination you can think of. How can you calculate this figure? It is a guesstimate. There are some analytics companies that provide sentiment analysis and are attempting to crack relevancy; however, they are not quite to the level where we feel comfortable using them inside of Intellifluence's influencer discovery tool[37]. Assign a relevancy percentage based on profile page, on recent posts, whatever you want—but be reasonable. If I mention "yoga" once every few months on Twitter, I'm not 100 percent relevant to yoga, but I might be 20 percent based on my perceived expertise and what I share with my audience.

COST

Cost is cost. In most cases at Intellifluence, the cost for the brand[38] is just the product cost plus shipping. In some cases, when negotiating with an influencer, you might need to offer money as well, but this situation is rarer than it is common. The reason I like to show cost here is because it is the biggest balancer on audience reach. Typically, much larger audiences charge a lot more money.

LET'S SEE THIS IN ACTION!

Consider two, non-randomly chosen examples: Joe S. and Damien T.

I know Damien, so I hope he doesn't mind this playful comparison.

---

[37] Intellifluence (2016). Find the right influencers and make more sales. Retrieved from https://intellifluence.com/discover?geo=all&network=all&category=all

[38] Intellifluence (2016). Hello, brands. Retrieved from https://intellifluence.com/brands

Joe S.

Damien T.

Who should you choose if you were picking between Damien and me? It depends.

Example 1: Selling deadlift bars on Twitter

Joe S. Outcome = (Audience (3,636) * Engagement (80%) * Relevance (20%)—$250 [cost of product + shipping guess])

Joe S. Outcome = 331.76

Damien T. Outcome = (Audience (41,400) * Engagement (90%) * Relevance (2%)—$250 [cost of product + shipping])

Damien T. Outcome = 495.2

Even though I might be more relevant than Damien on matters related to deadlifts, because he has such a large audience that engages with him, it might make more sense to have him review the product. This scenario is a prime example of using peer influencers with large audiences for generalized products.

Example 2: Influencer marketing SaaS toolset

Joe S. Outcome = (Audience (3,636) * Engagement (80%) * Relevance (100%)—$0 [digital products!])

Joe S. Outcome = 2,908.8

Damien T. Outcome = (Audience (41,400) * Engagement (90%) * Relevance (7%)—$0)

Damien T. Outcome = 2,608.2

Damien is probably more relevant than 7 percent, but I wanted to highlight an example of where relevance is going to win out over raw audience size. Had I assumed a 10 percent for

Damien, he'd have once again placed ahead of me and I'd be crying into my beer.

WHY CHOOSE?

The conundrum of the above scenario is based on a potentially faulty assumption of having to choose. Feasibly, so long as the outcome is a positive number, there is a benefit to engaging with both Joe and Damien. This situation is true for both examples but particularly on matters of influencer marketing. If you had 20 sample products that could be provided and found 20 somewhat relevant influencers with decent audience sizes, it'd most likely be in your best interest to engage with all of them. This reality is doubly true for those of you selling digital products. If there's no real cost associated by offering a free version, then you almost want to engage with as many influencers as you possibly can—the reality is that any positive review will be beneficial, of course not accounting for the time investment.

Photo 8.1. Credit: Kaboompics

CHAPTER 8

How to Pitch Influencers

Pitching influencers is like selling any product or service. With that analogy, learn the difference between cold and warm influencer outreach as well as how to create a good, converting pitch that provides value. Next, get an explanation of how to adjust the pitch during testing and a closing plea on the importance of being responsive as a function of successfully closing the pitch.

By now, you have a good idea of what your goal is[39] , you know who you are ultimately trying to influence[40], you have picked the social channels[41] you're going to start with, and, at this point, you have a list of which product reviewing influencers[42] you want to work with. The difference between knowing what you want to accomplish and actually succeeding is the next gap: You need to outreach. You need to pitch.

COLD VS. WARM OUTREACH

I've been in sales positions for much of my life, and a CEO is always selling. Thus, when I have the option between cold outreach and warm outreach, the comparison isn't even close. My success ratio is going to be exponentially better on the warm leads. As an example, if you built your contact list using a tool like Buzzstream, you have been building a cold outreach lead list and will need to take a slightly different campaign approach than if you're reaching out to individuals that are already in the mindset of wanting to do product reviews[43] as an influencer.

To keep this topic relatively concise, I'll oversimplify: When performing cold outreach, the importance of the subject title and obvious value exchange are going to be even higher than if you are reaching out to a warm lead. Additionally, one needs to adopt an expectation that more than one outreach will be required. In complex sales cycles to cold leads, it was not uncommon for me to send more than six emails over several months just trying to get the attention of a prospect and providing unique value in each email. It was also not uncommon for a sale to occur on the first pitch to a warm lead. The difference is that significant.

WHAT CONSTITUTES A GOOD PITCH?

Operating now on the assumption that you've signed up[44] on a service like Intellifluence where influencers have joined[45] the network (that is, potential warm leads), let's focus on what makes for a good pitch.

CONVERTING COPY. You have only one chance to make that first impression. Don't squander it with a boring subject line like "please review my product" and 17 paragraphs on why the influencer should be falling over themselves trying to get a free sample. It doesn't work, and the psychology is backwards. In your message body, you need to play to the ego

---

[39] Sinkwitz, J. (2016, September 28). How to set goals for your influencer campaign. Retrieved from https://blog.intellifluence.com/how-to-set-goals-for-your-influencer-campaign-abc236257f79

[40] Sinkwitz, J. (2016, October 5). Who exactly are your trying to influence? Retrieved from https://blog.intellifluence.com/who-are-you-trying-to-influence-ba8ddaf5a575

[41] Sinkwitz, J. (2016, October 11). Which social channel will bring sales for your business? Retrieved from https://blog.intellifluence.com/which-social-channel-will-bring-sales-for-your-business-c8831fb0c4e2

[42] Sinkwitz, J. (2016, October 26). Time to pick the right product influencers. Retrieved from https://blog.intellifluence.com/time-to-pick-the-right-product-influencers-531c13ed49a1

[43] Intellifluencer (2016). Find the right influencers and make more sales. Retrieved from https://intellifluence.com/discover?geo=all&network=all&category=all

[44] Intellifluence (2016). Brands, try us for free. Retrieved from https://intellifluence.com/register

[45] Intellifluence (2016). Welcome, influencers. Retrieved from https://intellifluence.com/influencers/

of the influencers, explain why THEY are perfect for the product, and overcome objections by stating upfront what you're willing to offer in exchange for their time. As for titles, incredible copywriters like Joel K can teach you books worth about the hook and the reel, but suffice it to say, you need that colorful lure in the subject that should probably be unique for each campaign at worst and unique for each influencer at best. Example? If you were reaching out to my influencer profile for the purposes of having me review kitten socks, be absurd: "Want to increase your deadlift? Review my knee-high kitten socks." And, oh yes, it happened [46]. If the hook is really good, you can almost get away with a weaker value exchange, but since you are trying to maximize the sheer number of quality reviews in order to increase sales, we can't overlook it.

Photo 8.2. Credit: Hannah Wei

VALUE EXCHANGE. In your initial outreach copy, you need to be explicit, and if you know you're trying to get busy influencers to work with you instead of spending their time reviewing someone else's product, you need to stand out. Yes, the majority of the influencers[47] in our network are willing to review in exchange for product, but the bigger the audience and more sophisticated and in-depth the review, the more willing you need to be to value that person's time and, thus, offer more value. This review can come in the way of cold hard cash. It can come by promising to highlight that review for a guaranteed level of additional exposure. It can be done by offering a larger lot of product. It can be done in the red paperclip method[48] by exchanging something the influencer wants as a means of leveling up to the influence you need. Whatever that value exchange is, don't be stingy—if you know you're reaching out to someone who reviews beauty products for a living and has been known to drive traffic, you're setting yourself up for failure by trying to lowball with a small amount of product, no cash, and less value than the influencer might be getting elsewhere. Determining the right mix of value of offer can be tricky, which is why we test.

---

[46] Retrieved from https://twitter.com/CygnusSEO/status/773939680165306368

[47] Intellifluence (2016). Welcome, influencers. Retrieved from https://intellifluence.com/influencers

[48] Retrieved from http://oneredpaperclip.blogspot.com/

TEST, TEST, TEST

The reality is you might find yourself in a situation where no one responds to you on some pitches and everyone responds to you on other pitches. The former is of course undesirable, but in some cases, the latter should be tweaked to optimize your overall spend. Let's talk about when and how to change up your pitches using a bit of logic.

IF you get no responses to your pitch, THEN first change your subject to be catchier.

ELSE IF you have already modified your subject, then you need to drastically change your message to focus more on the influencer and increase the value exchange. Remember: Don't ask the influencer to jump through a lot of hoops, contact you outside of the system, or otherwise make life difficult. The simpler and more straightforward the task, with obvious value exchange, the higher probability of success will be.

IF you get responses to your pitch but no acceptances, THEN improve the value exchange. In this scenario, you're at least getting the attention of influencers, but you need to compel them to want to work with you.

ELSE IF you have already increased value, THEN reconsider who you are pitching to. Go back to make sure you're targeting the right type of influencer[49] and have picked the right target list[50] for that type.

ELSE IF you have increased value and ensured you're contacting the right people, THEN ease up on the requirements of your pitch. It is possible you are simply asking for too much and the influencers perceive it as too much of a headache.

IF you have 100 percent acceptance, THEN consider lowering what you're offering for the next round. I don't intend to mean that you should be stingy, but it is possible that you may be offering too much and can afford to lower the amount of product or other value offered and still get an overwhelmingly positive response.

ELSE IF you have 100 percent and can't lower the value offered any further, THEN ask for more in the way of reviews. It could be an additional post, a follow-up interview with the reviewer for your blog, etc.

IF you have a greater than 50 percent higher acceptance rate AND you're only offering product, THEN play with changing the subject and messaging on each round of outreach to see if you can increase the number of reviews you're getting, without having to give up any more value.

As you can see, there is always room to improve and test, and to help you find the balance

---

[49] Sinkwitz, J. (2016, October 18). Determining the right influencer type for your campaign. Retrieved from https://blog.intellifluence.com/determining-the-right-influencer-type-for-your-campaign-837a8fe94ff2

[50] Sinkwitz, J. (2016, October 26). Time to pick the right product influencers. Retrieved from https://blog.intellifluence.com/time-to-pick-the-right-product-influencers-531c13ed49a1

on receiving a strong number of reviews that result in sales without having to offer up more than is necessary to accomplish the task.

BE RESPONSIVE

As a final note, be responsive. One characteristic that makes for an excellent reviewer is to not only follow directions, but to do so in a punctual manner. The same goes for brands[51]. As much as you are considering and deciding on which influencers to choose, they equally deliberate on which brands to work with. It can be as simple as getting back to influencers within the day that a question is asked. Brands that are quick to respond to questions will earn more attention and a higher overall close rate. Similar to making this process analogous to sales, if you want an action to occur (that is, a reviewer to accept your pitch), you need to strike when that individual is ready to take action.

Now go pitch!

---

[51] Intellifluence (2016). Hello, brands. Retrieved from https://intellifluence.com/brands

Photo 9.1. Credit: Khara Woods

CHAPTER 9

Local vs. National: Which Influencer Audience Type Is Better?

Learn when you should opt for a local influencer vs. a less geographically centric influencer. A usefulness matrix exists to determine the importance of location by exploring geocentricity, geobias, geospecificity, and geoactivity. To explain varying scenarios, case studies for Starwars.com, Miami Fishing Charters, and BloomNation are used.

In order to answer this question, you're going to need to understand what it is you're trying to accomplish. This chapter is Chapter 9, so before digging in on whether local or national influencer audiences matter more for you and your campaign, do the following:

1. Set goals[52] for your campaign.

2. Understand who[53] you are trying to influence.

3. Pick the appropriate social channels[54].

4. Select the type of influencer[55] who ties into overall campaign goals.

Now that you're caught up, here's my answer to this complex question: It depends. Since there are multiple variables that go into determining the types of audiences that are ideal for your campaign, let's kick off with our favorite educational method.

GEO AUDIENCE USEFULNESS MATRIX

For this matrix, we'll be looking into whether certain attributes are served better by local audiences or by national audiences and trying to answer yes (Y) or no (N) questions as a way of making that determination (except for geoactivity). Bear with me as this discussion is probably going to be new terminology:

1. **GEOCENTRICITY.** Are the buyer personas chosen for the campaign confined primarily to a specific geographic? Example: Buyer persona is a mom in Phoenix and only buys local. National exposure may be overkill if the buyer is always local.

2. **GEOBIAS.** Would tying to a specific local audience inherently alienate other geographies? Example: Selling Boston Red Sox hats is a 100 percent good idea for the Boston market, but not so good in New York City.

3. **GEOSPECIFICITY.** Is your business confined to a single or small set of locations? Example: A chain of grocery stores is within a 50-mile radius. While this point may seem like an obvious consideration, you'd be surprised how often national advertising is purchased for small businesses who cannot serve outside of a relatively fixed geographic boundary. Geospecificity is essentially the mirror of egocentricity; one is buyer focused and one is seller focused.

4. **GEOACTIVITY.** Is the campaign goal skewed more toward awareness or engagement? National campaigns support national awareness and local campaigns

---

[52] Sinkwitz, J. (2016, September 28). How to set goals for your influencer campaign. Retrieved https://blog.intellifluence.com/how-to-set-goals-for-your-influencer-campaign-abc236257f79

[53] Sinkwitz, J. (2016, October 5). Who exactly are you trying to influence? Retrieved from https://blog.intellifluence.com/who-are-you-trying-to-influence-ba8ddaf5a575

[54] Sinkwitz, J. (2016, October 11). Which social channel will bring sales for your business? Retrieved from https://blog.intellifluence.com/which-social-channel-will-bring-sales-for-your-business-c8831fb0c4e2

[55] Sinkwitz, J. (2016, October 18). Determining the right influencer type for your campaign. Retrieved from https://blog.intellifluence.com/determining-the-right-influencer-type-for-your-campaign-837a8fe94ff2

support local awareness. However, research from Howard Lerman of Yext shows that local tagging in Instagram influencer campaigns led to 70 percent higher engagement. Hat tip to Andrew Shotland for pointing me to this area. In my opinion, it reinforces the importance of peer influence on local levels and is going to be something we push to improve on for influencer discovery[56].

Now that we understand the types of questions we need to ask, let's see how the local vs. national audience question plays out over a few different case studies.

CASE STUDY 1: STARWARS.COM

- For Jeff Preston of Disney, parent company of Starwars.com
- Product: Disney Infinity 3.0 Edition

Buyer persona: A 24-year-old female living in Los Angeles named Karen is a huge Rey fan. She is an Android phone user, and with any downtime, she can be found posting on gaming forums with her support of the Rebel Alliance.

TYPE	Geocentricity	Geobias	Geospecificity	Geoactivity
Karen	N	N	N	Awareness

Graphic 9.1. Source: Intellifluence

In this particular case, a local campaign wouldn't be necessary. Karen is willing to purchase and view content from any local so long as it is Star Wars related. She isn't going to be bothered by Phoenix Star Wars events showing in an influencer campaign as they are not competing geographies. If anything, if the content provided is on localized events, she'll likely judge whether it is worth the trip to attend. As Starwars.com is not tied to a fixed location, it needn't worry about local campaigns if the purpose of the campaign is to generate awareness with the understanding that awareness will lead to the desired engagement action anyhow.

CASE STUDY 2: MIAMI FISHING CHARTERS

- For Todd Malicoat, owner of Miami Fishing Charters
- Product: Miami area fishing charter

Buyer persona: A 38-year-old male living in Phoenix named Joe has never been big-game fishing, but he wants to learn. He knows he needs to travel to a place where big fish exist since Arizona is landlocked until California inevitably falls into the ocean, and he happens to have a few days of dead time in the Miami area.

TYPE	Geocentricity	Geobias	Geospecificity	Geoactivity
Joe	Y	N	Y	Engagement

[56] Intellifluence (2016) Find the right influencers and make more sales. Retrieved from https://intellifluence.com/discover?geo=all&network=all&category=all

For Joe, he's going to be in Miami (or is already there). He wants to make a decision on big-game fishing for his specified days, but doesn't care so much if he sees content for another area (although it wouldn't be as useful to him). Since Miami Fishing Charters appears to be focused on the Miami area with the location of the Marauder, and the goal is to get charters booked, a local campaign is going to make obvious sense. For the engagement boost, those campaigns are going to be appropriately tagged by satisfied customers.

CASE STUDY 3: BLOOMNATION

- For Eric Wu, VP of Product for BloomNation

- Product: flower delivery

Buyer persona: A 45-year-old male living in New York City named Steve forgot his anniversary and is buying emergency flowers, stat! The flowers need to be perfect; he can't afford any more mistakes with chain flower bouquets that never end up looking right.

TYPE	Geocentricity	Geobias	Geospecificity	Geoactivity
Steve	Y	Y	Y	Engagement

This example is actually a trick case study. While BloomNation obviously has national appeal and national coverage, each geographic area's bouquets are unique. This assertion means that the product needs to be treated as though it is a single location area, for the buyer's perspective. Steve needs flowers fast, so seeing only New York City relevant flowers is key, and something that looks local looks better than a chain. The expected Instagram engagement with location tagging would be rather high.

TO LOCAL OR NOT TO LOCAL, IT TOTALLY DEPENDS … IS THE ANSWER

As you can see, similar to picking the right social channels and influencer types, the decision to focus on influencers with local audiences can be pretty important for some campaigns. If you are selling to a geographically constrained audience, opting for local level influencers to make use of relevant local tagging might make all the difference for your campaign.

Photo 10 1 Credit: Jan Vašek

CHAPTER 10

So You Got Your First Review; Now What?

After a review is received, there's a process to undertake to ensure that the review meets the criteria agreed upon in the pitch, whether revisions by the influencer are required, and promotional strategies to use (co-opting content, audience engagement, amplification, retargeting, native advertising, and email) to ensure maximum value is achieved with the review.

Someone reviewed your product. Well, isn't that special.

No matter if you followed any specific targeting advice on picking the right influencer[57] based on buyer personas[58], social channel[59] selection, or influencer type[60] needs, here you are, ready for Chapter 10. If you have a review, you apparently nailed the pitch[61].

NOW WHAT?

First, let's look into the basics of the review before moving any further.

1. Does your product or brand URL exist? I would hope this one is obvious, but having thumbed through way more social reviews that I can count at this point, it is important to point out—branded experiences are fine, but for the love of your bottom line, you should be getting some direct traffic benefit from this approach. In other words, a link should exist. For those platforms that make embedding links difficult in the post itself, a link should exist in the first available comment by the reviewer.

2. Is the review factual? Note that I'm not asking on whether the review is "good" or "positive"— just the facts, ma'am. This item would include imagery of the product, how it is described, described features ... you don't want a situation where your paid review could be construed as false advertising. The FTC[62] pays close attention to this sort of practice when significant sales volume is associated with the tactic, so if someone is misled, it can come back to hurt you.

3. Is the review tagged (where applicable)? While this item isn't nearly as important as having your URL in an accurate review, it still matters, especially for discovery purposes on platforms like Twitter and Instagram where a significant portion of the traffic occurs via hashtag queries and is important for discovery purposes.

If everything looks great, you can skip to what to do next from a promotional point of view. However, what if it isn't? What's your recourse?

---

[57] Sinkwitz, J. (2016, October 26). Time to pick the right product influencers. Retrieved from https://blog.intellifluence.com/time-to-pick-the-right-product-influencers-531c13ed49a1

[58] Sinkwitz, J. (2016, September 19). Why should influencer marketing be a part of your strategy? Retrieved from https://blog.intellifluence.com/why-should-influencer-marketing-be-a-part-of-your-strategy-88122ece9dab

[59] Sinkwitz, J. (2016, October 11). Which social channel will bring sales for your business? Retrieved from https://blog.intellifluence.com/which-social-channel-will-bring-sales-for-your-business-c8831fb0c4e2

[60] Sinkwitz, J. (2016, October 18). Determining the right influencer type for your campaign. Retrieved from https://blog.intellifluence.com/determining-the-right-influencer-type-for-your-campaign-837a8fe94ff2

[61] Sinkwitz, J. (2016, October 31). How to pitch influencers. Retrieved from https://blog.intellifluence.com/how-to-pitch-influencers-5b2dd319a0c6

[62] Federal Trade Commission (n.d.). Division of advertising practices. Retrieved from https://www.ftc.gov/about-ftc/bureaus-offices/bureau-consumer-protection/our-divisions/division-advertising-practices

WHEN TO ASK FOR REVISIONS

In our platform, brands[63] have the ability to request modifications on reviews; however, it is important to point out that modifications should only be used in certain cases.

1. If the review is missing information (that is, your link), then you'd have an obvious reason to request a change, a change that 99 pecent of influential reviews aren't going to have a problem with. Don't try to force the issue of dofollow vs. nofollow links though. Technically, if the link is paid for in product or compensation, then a nofollow link is appropriate.

2. If the review is not factual, you definitely need to get it fixed. If the reviewer used imagery for the wrong product, said that it has capabilities that it does not, or is quoting an inaccurate price, request for a fix. Sadly, this situation usually occurs due to laziness or rushed timelines, but if you're straightforward and honest in your intentions on why you're requesting a change, the reviewer will most likely do it.

3. If what was agreed to isn't completed. If you negotiated with an influencer[64] on the length and depth of a review, what type of review it is (shoutout vs. product review vs. background use), or social channel selection, then you have a valid reason to request a change. This point is especially true if you are providing more product or compensation than the initial pitch in exchange for an above-and-beyond experience. We have a granular option to request changes on a URL post level rather than having to reject an entire campaign, but regardless of which platform you're getting reviews through, it is important for both buyer and seller to fulfill their obligations.

4. Don't ask for revision just because you aren't happy with the opinion expressed by an influencer. Honesty and transparency is extremely important; don't try to suppress it. The best way to treat such reviews is to acknowledge whatever shortcomings may exist and iterate on the product, then reach out again in the future to get an updated review.

Assuming now that you've made it through the needed revisions, it is time to make the review work for you.

PROMOTE IT!

One thing I've learned in my couple decades of SEO and content marketing is that no single piece of promotion or content should exist in a vacuum. Since you've worked so hard to get your first review, you try to amplify your outcome as best as possible, borrowing from some compulsion marketing[65] techniques.

---

[63] Intellifluence (2016). Hello, brands. Retrieved from https://intellifluence.com/brands

[64] Intellifluence (2016). Welcome, influencers. Retrieved from https://intellifluence.com/influencers/

[65] Intellifluence (2016). Compulsion marketing: Making your campaign irresistible. Retrieved from https://www.slideshare.net/intellifluence/compulsion-marketing-making-your-campaign-irresistible

Co-opt. With permission of the reviewer, what can you transfer to your own blog or social channels? For example:

1. If you received an in-depth YouTube review, embed it into your blog and promote your blog post to give both you and your reviewer more exposure.

2. Consider posting in multiple mediums. In that video, slice it into multiple postings for Instagram stories or snaps, take still images from the video to be used as social proof on your landing pages, and in Pinterest, repost the video into Facebook and Twitter native formats.

3. If the video didn't have a transcription, add it to your blog to increase the value of the content.

4. Build out mega content. In other words, if you were to get five different video reviews, you could incorporate them into a blog series that you could later circulate to your prospects via email.

Photo 10.2. Credit: Startup Stock Photos

Engage. It goes without saying that you should like, favorite, retweet, share, comment, and show your support for your reviewers.

Amplify. There are three ways to think about amplifying, and I'll use Twitter as the social channel example:

1. Amplify the review via advertising to your audience [what most brands tend to do].

2. Amplify the review via advertising to your reviewers' audience [this action is what smarter brands do].

3. Amplify the review to an expanded look-alike audience to your reviewers' audience [this activity is what even smarter brands do].

4. Do all of the above [this is what I do].

Retarget. This topic can get quite a bit complicated, but there are a variety of ways to think about this area.

1. You can upload visitor cookies into a variety of uptake channels, like Google, via an extended audience targeting.

2. You can iterate on the amplification strategy above and export the list, if you can slip in a pixel, to target on channels that you haven't even yet focused on.

3. Hire an agency like Tony Adam's Visible Factors to handle the paid targeting.

Native. One of the benefits of co-opting great reviews as content on your own site is that native advertising networks will generally only allow content-rich pages as approved landing pages. You can thinking of native as a mashup between display advertising and retargeting because you can do the following:

1. Only target to a retargeting list.

2. Expand to target your buyer persona demographic for more top-of-sales funnel expansion.

Email. I absolutely love email. If you have a great review, wouldn't you want to share it with your list of prospects who haven't yet decided to purchase from you? One of your secondary goals in selling products needs to be to build an email list. I cannot emphasize this point enough—nothing is more effective to get the word out when you're launching new products, having a sale, or wishing to communicate to your base. There are two main options here:

1. Use a segmenting email tool like Customer.io or Getdrip.com to manage your prospecting list, relying on logic to determine how to push a person from initial desire and awareness down into purchasing mode. Another new tool that shows promise is Sujan Patel's Mailshake.

2. Use a managed email service like FireDrum[66].

NEXT?

After you get a great review and promote it, you'll likely see the benefits in terms of an increase in sales attributed to your social channels. After you do this step, keep going! The beauty of peer-level product reviews is that when compared to other marketing activities, they are very affordable. The more, the merrier.

---

[66] FireDrum (n.d.). Full service email marketing pricing. Retrieved from https://www.firedrumemailmarketing.com/email-marketing-full-service-program/

Photo 11.1. Credit: Valeria Boltneva

CHAPTER 11

Influencer Negotiation: What Is Fair?

Is it worth it to negotiate with an influencer? That answer depends entirely on the perceived value exchange. If negotiation is necessary, choose between a relational and transactional approach. Finally, learn how to negotiate with the influencer using the Harvard Business Review nine-step guide to negotiation (determine satisfactory outcome, identify opportunities to create mutual value, identify your BATNA, improve your BATNA, get the decision maker, prepare, adapt as necessary, establish fairness, and alter the process if necessary).

You led with a pitch to the influencer[67], and because you understood the appropriate value assignment and picked the right product influencers[68], it was a solid pitch.

However, you find yourself now with a reply from an influencer asking for more. What to do, what to do? If you're lost already, please review the previous chapters. Why? I want you to get the full benefit of this chapter. At minimum, review the other two chapters referenced on selecting the best influencers and pitching them if you're struggling with any of the concepts thus far. [69]

IS IT WORTH IT?

The first question as you see the reply in front of you is whether or not negotiation is worth your time. Should you simply move on to different influencers or continue the conversation?

1. If you applied the rough mathematics associated with picking the right product influencers, then your target is of the best possible fit for you. In such a case, I would advise at least continuing with the process.

2. If you applied more of a scattershot approach and have contacted a large number of influencers on your campaign, then you may be all right politely declining to pay more and give more. Just don't ignore the message; that isn't professional.

PICKING A NEGOTIATION STRATEGY

The next consideration is how you anticipate using influencers and influencer networks like Intellifluence in the future. There are two primary schools of thought: relational negotiating and transactional negotiating. Let's explore the differences.

Relational. Long-term focused, viewing the current transaction as one of a series of many future transactions. The focus is less on haggling and more on choice selection, where trust is more important than time expended in making that choice. If the transaction is successful, a repeat transaction is likely, and it's important in businesses where word of mouth is crucial.

Transactional. Short-term focused, where the future transactions are less of a consideration. The focus is on today's deal and haggling for the best one. Trust and loyalty aren't nearly as strong of factors; this style of negotiating is more about winning. If the other party

Daddy needs a new pair of shoes!

Graphic 11.1 Source: Intellifluence

[67] Sinkwitz, J. (2016, October 31). How to pitch influencers. Retrieved from https://blog.intellifluence.com/how-to-pitch-influencers-5b2dd319a0c6

[68] Sinkwitz, J. (2016, October 26). Time to pick the right product influencers. Retrieved from https://blog.intellifluence.com/time-to-pick-the-right-product-influencers-531c13ed49a1

[69] Sinkwitz, J. (2016, September 13). What is influencer marketing? Retrieved from https://blog.intellifluence.com/what-is-influencer-marketing-40549fe706b4

perceives a win, then a strong word-of-mouth marketing takes places to other similar negotiators.

Which is right for influencer marketing though? On one hand, if you have a successful campaign, you'll want to be able to use the same influencer again for follow-ups, future product launches, etc. On the other hand, let's make a stronger assumption: If you're reading this, you may have discovered some influencers[70] and pitched, not fully knowing what to expect as a ROI. Thus, in order to even consider employing the strategy back, you need a win.

To make this work as well as possible, we're going to approach this negotiation as a polite transactional, which leaves the door open in the future for a greater relationship to flourish. In order to do this, let's employ the Harvard Business Review's nine steps to getting the deal done.

Step 1: Determine satisfactory outcome for the influencer review.

On your end, the satisfactory outcome would be a review on the right social channels[71] that deliver traffic that converts into sales. How many sales? For your reviewer? An appropriate compensation for the time expended. At this stage, you don't yet know what the appropriate compensation is—hence the negotiation.

Step 2: Identify the opportunities to create value

This phase is the common ground phase. You more or less have already covered that area. Both parties believe the product is worth reviewing and the influencer[72] is worth receiving some form of compensation for his or her time.

Step 3: Identify your BATNA and reservation price

A BATNA is the **Best Alternative to Negotiated Agreement**. Given the type of transaction we're discussing, your BATNA could be to give the same amount of product and compensation to the next influencer on your list or it could be to spend the money on PPC or any number of activities. Knowing the highest price you'll pay and your alternative if a deal can't be reached that fits within those parameters is key, but so is trying to determine the other party's BATNA. If the influencer declines the review at your current offer levels, is there another review waiting to be handled? Is the influencer highly sought after and thus is always busy? Or, is the alternative more free time? These areas are important considerations.

---

[70] Intellifluence (2016). Find the right influencers and make more sales. Retrieved from https://intellifluence.com/discover?geo=all&network=all&category=all

[71] Sinkwitz, J. (2016, October 11). Which social channel will bring sales for your business? Retrieved from https://blog.intellifluence.com/which-social-channel-will-bring-sales-for-your-business-c8831fb0c4e2

[72] Intellifluence (2016). Hello, influencers. Retrieved from https://intellifluence.com/influencers/

Step 4: Improve your BATNA

It goes without saying that the better your alternative is, the stricter you can be in your current negotiations. As an example, continue researching other influencers that might actually be a better fit and at better pricing, and continue testing other forms of traffic (always test — forever test).

Step 5: Get the decision maker

For all intents and purposes, the influencer responding to your pitch is the decision maker. However, that approach isn't always the case. It is possible that the pitch and negotiation is being handled by an assistant—a caveat before you attempt to circumvent, the process may exist for a reason and attempts to bypass might result in burning a bridge. If you feel very strongly about the deal offered, believe it is also perfect for the influencer. If you have determined that you aren't getting anywhere with the support staff, then you may have nothing to lose by approaching directly via social channels to indicate how excited you are to be working with said influencer in the future, if terms can be met.

Photo 11.2. Credit: Startup Stock Photos

Step 6: Study like the test is tomorrow

The more you know about your counterparty the better. Granted, you may not have time to invest in this idea, but assuming that this item was an aspirational influencer pitch, it would be vital to understand the influencer's personality, negotiating style, cultural background, goals ... essentially anything that might impact a decision maker's thought process. The more you understand, the easier it'll be to understand your counterparty's BATNA and help to frame your offer in a way that exceeds that BATNA while remaining within your own scope of success.

Step 7: Prepare for process flexibility

Essentially, this stage is where you are. You pitched and received a counter, perhaps unexpectedly. Negotiations don't always follow the same volley of counters back and forth; sometimes strange and unpleasant situations arise out of emotional misunderstandings that can derail the overall process. Maybe someone else takes over negotiation for the influencer; maybe the counter keeps increasing instead of narrowing to something you'd be willing to pay. Patience is key. Be calm, collected, and firm with regards to your reservation price and BATNA, yet creative enough to find a solution that wins for everyone.

Step 8: Establish fairness

If the deal is to work, both parties need to be happy that the deal on the table (er ... inbox)

THE ULTIMATE GUIDE TO USING INFLUENCER MARKETING

is both fair and reasonable. If you were to research current and comparable rates for similar review types and audience sizes — which might go a long ways to helping the influencer understand that you aren't trying to take advantage of the situation — but instead you want to pay a fair price. Your criteria for fairness may not be the same as the influencer though, so be prepared to explain why your formula is the preferred method. Conversely, if the influencer is able to counter with even better criteria and data than you currently have, you may feel hard-pressed to reject the proposal and thus feel more satisfied with the proposed deal.

Step 9: Alter the process

The inverse of Step 7, if you feel that your ideas and criteria are being ignored, you can always alter the process in your favor by bringing in one of your own support staff to complete the transaction with limited knowledge only on price you're willing to pay and number and type of reviews you're willing to accept. Sometimes, changing who sits at the table can more readily result in a deal.

NEGOTIATE WITH AN EYE TO THE FUTURE

Just remember throughout the process to remain positive and focused on the goal of working with the influencer, including possibly again in the future. As such, be helpful in providing information, explaining your position, and if you are stuck, consider sharing why you are pitching with the product quantity and compensation levels that you are based on the criteria you used to determine what success might look like.

Photo 12.1. Credit: Clem Onojeghuo

CHAPTER 12

How to Maximize Exposure on Your Product Reviews

Using the compulsion marketing concept (pairing marketing tactics in order to use different psychological triggers: (aspirational influence, authoritative influence, peer influence, retargeting + social CPM/PPC, mega content campaigns, and email), learn how to maximize product review exposure through case studies for Bose and Ulta Beauty.

Chapter 12 already? The assumption for this chapter is that you've already received your first review[73]. If you aren't quite there yet, I recommend starting at the beginning[74]. What we're going to be focusing on in this chapter is trying to get the best ROI possible from those existing reviews. Compulsion marketing concepts work synergistically, so the sum of their parts ends up having a greater total impact that measuring those individual pieces separately—that's the thesis behind our attempts to take that existing review and make it more special.

COMPULSION MARKETING

First presented[75] at Unggaged, the concept is always undergoing evolution as more data becomes available, but suffice to say the entire point is to look into the psychological triggers used by marketers and attempt to order in such a way that mirrors a buying funnel, to guide a new user from awareness to sales.

Without getting into the specific psychological drivers associated with different influencer types[76], we'll focus instead on some of the marketing concepts that are utilized. As a refresher these include the following: aspirational influencers, authoritative influencer, peer influencers, retargeting + social CPM/PPC, mega content campaigns, and email.

The best way I learn is through example, so rather than lecture, let's try to build out two real-world case studies. Note: Intellifluence does not have relations with either company (yet?) so we aren't aware how much of what we propose might already be planned.

CASE STUDY 1 — BOSE

Presumably this section would be for Timothy Johnson of Bose, whose headphones campaign caught my eye when I found this review:

Photo 12.2. Credit: Twitter

Carolina Panthers @Panthers
RT for chance to win these @Bose headphones!
We'll pick a random winner by 7PM. #QC35
#35DaysofQC #ad http://bose.life/XgThY
4:34 PM - 5 Dec 2016

- 62 Replies
- 2,199 Retweets
- 465 Likes

---

[73] Sinkwitz, J. (2016, November 22). So you got your first review; now what? Retrieved from https://blog.intellifluence.com/so-you-got-your-first-review-now-what-13df54960fbf

[74] Sinkwitz, J. (2016, September 13). What is influencer marketing? Retrieved from https://blog.intellifluence.com/what-is-influencer-marketing-40549fe706b4

[75] Intellifluence (2016). Compulsion marketing: Making your campaign irresistible. Retrieved from https://www.slideshare.net/intellifluence/compulsion-marketing-making-your-campaign-irresistible

[76] Sinkwitz, J. (2016, October 18). Determining the right influencer type for your campaign. Retrieved from https://blog.intellifluence.com/determining-the-right-influencer-type-for-your-campaign-837a8fe94ff2

Bose headphones is in the middle of a campaign with many if not all NFL Twitter channels. It's pretty neat, just based on reach alone, since each NFL channel is hosting a mini review of the product. Clearly, there's a lot going on, so how would I go about trying to turn this into something more?

1. Twitter's specialty ad formats are the first thing that comes to mind. Ads that appear to be organically sourced vs. forced have much higher engagement rates, so one of the first moves would be for Bose to schedule regular promoted tweets on the various NFL accounts to continually appeal to those audiences.

2. The other ad option worth discussing with regards to Twitter is the look-alike audiences. Promoting to look-alike followers of specific NFL teams, fenced geographically to prevent fan base overlap, Bose can expand its awareness footprint further and collect the cookies for a future part of the campaign.

3. Contact Dennis Goedegebuure of Fanatics about creating a co-branded NFL ultimate super fan apparel and audiophile experience: UGC videos and blog posts with giveaways and contents galore, with requests to reference the original NFL review tweets for amplification.

4. Contact Kelly Dunne at CBS Sports to creatively retarget both the initial NFL promotion, look-alike promotion, and Fanatics co-branded super fan experience across their sports site portfolio, specifically amplifying the personal stories (which will in turn end up amplifying the original reviews).

5. Create audience network ads in Facebook and Instagram for the various campaigns. Since Instagram now supports it, integrate the buy button and adopt a direct sales approach on these ads.

6. Work further with CBS to syndicate the ads out to the broader network.

7. Drip email to anyone that entered the flow moving from celebrity player reviews -> NFL team reviews -> super fan reviews. Near the end of the drip campaign, offer a sizeable coupon if the buyer engages on social media about why they want Bose headphones to complete their NFL experience.

CASE STUDY 2 — ULTA BEAUTY

Presumably this would be for Eric Messerschmidt of Ulta Beauty, who is already doing some of the Twitter amplification strategies I'd recommend. The tweet below is actually an example of Ulta promoting an existing review — kudos.

VICKYLOGAN @victoriouslogan

Thank you @ultabeauty for gifting me your holiday beauty box to spread #joytothegirl!

#JoyItForward http://Ultabeauty.com/joy #ad
3:53 PM - 16 Nov 2016

- 4 Replies
- 43 Retweets
- 450 Likes

1. The next step I would recommend is to aggressively backfill with peer reviews[77]. Rather than having the peer reviewers post their own reviews, instead provide product and existing review URLs and ask to retweet that URL, including their own 140-character review of the product with it. This approach would allow Ulta to skip directly to the wealth drivers phase and unity psychological triggers. The impression becomes that of a pack mentality, where everyone seems to be using the product.

2. Given this item is beauty, which is obviously visual, let's include the right social networks[78]: Instagram and Pinterest. Using the same techniques used on Twitter, use a handful of authoritative influencers and then backfill with peer reviewers to amplify those initial reviews with repinning and sharing.

3. For all the distinct campaigns, create Facebook audience network campaigns designed to target the desired buyer persona. Use dark posts first to determine which variations are the most successful and expand on the winning ads once that variation is determined.

4. Similar to Bose, a moderated UGC promotion campaign tied to the influencer campaign would create a deep series of review content that can be used to deep link into product pages, flowing social traffic, and some link equity.

5. Contact Dave Snyder at CopyPress to build out interactives on the best ways to use different cosmetics for skin type and hair type, sourcing sales data and UGC reviews for guidance, shuttling link equity once again from the entry point of the interactives into the most important product pages.

6. Kick off an outreach campaign to mommy bloggers with the intend of earning embeds on the interactive pieces created. At the end of the interactive flow, include a displayed coupon code that can be tied back to each mommy blogger for future affiliate relationships. Using a coupon code at the end of the interactive allows Ulta to treat these embeds like engaged display advertising.

[77] Intellifluence (2016). Find the right influencers and make more sales. Retrieved from https://intellifluence.com/discover?geo=all&network=all&category=all
[78] Sinkwitz, J. (2016, October 11) Which social channel will bring sales for your business? Retrieved from https://blog.intellifluence.com/which-social-channel-will-bring-sales-for-your-business-c8831fb0c4e2

These examples are just two sample campaigns that could be conceptualized using compulsion marketing concepts and carried out to maximize the exposure of the initial product reviews. Any brand[79] is capable of receiving this type of attention with the right amount of budget. For the more budget conscious, something is always better than nothing, and we're obviously big fans of saving money—in such a case, consider using peer reviewers to carry out amplification tasks for you.

[79] Intellifluence (2016). Hello, brands Retrieved from https://intellifluence.com/brands

Photo 13.1. Credit: Adrianna Calvo

CHAPTER 13

Round Two: Use the Same Reviewers or Get New Ones?

When deciding to utilize influencer marketing on a second campaign, one needs to decide whether to use the same influencers or find new ones. The decision to do so can be reached using a decision matrix that considers product uniqueness, product change, habitual use, ideal audience, the benefit of repetition, and the existence of new influencers to consider. To explain the concept, Frank Body is used as a case study.

Here's the scenario: You're back for more influencer marketing. Either the previous campaign went well, or it didn't and you know why it didn't. This strategy discussion will explore the best way to approach that second wave, regardless of what happened. If you're new to this idea and haven't had a first pass on using product reviewers for influencer marketing, do the following:

1. Figure out a buyer persona[80] for what you're selling. Sometimes this determination is hard, and you need to go deeper[81].

2. Determine the social network[82] best suited for your product.

3. Settle on the influencer type[83] needed to give you the most success (hint: probably a peer influencer).

4. Pick your product reviewers[84].

5. Pitch[85] those reviewers.

6. Come back here when you're done.

Can you guess how we at Intellifluence like to come up with the best strategy when it comes to a potentially complicated decision? That's right: We made a decision matrix!

REPLAY OR NEW GAME? DECISION MATRIX

Unique product. This question is looking to determine if you are going to be seeking reviews on the same exact product or an entirely different product. All things being equal, if the previous campaign was a success and the product is unique, there is a

	Yes	No
Unique product		
Not unique with change		
Habitual		
Ideal audience		
Repetition benefit		
New discovery		

Graphic 13.1. Source: Intellifluence

dual benefit to approaching a reviewer you worked with in the past. Not only do you know that the audience is receptive to the influence, but by repeating brand messaging, you are playing upon one of the core tenets of compulsion marketing by piling on. On the other hand, if the reviews sought are for the exact same product, the benefit of using the same

---

[80] Sinkwitz, J. (2016, September 19). Why should influencer marketing be a part of your strategy? Retrieved from https://blog.intellifluence.com/why-should-influencer-marketing-be-a-part-of-your-strategy-88122ece9dab

[81] Sinkwitz, J. (2016, October 5). Who exactly are you trying to influence? Retrieved from https://blog.intellifluence.com/who-are-you-trying-to-influence-ba8ddaf5a575

[82] Sinkwitz, J. (2016, October 11) Which social channel will bring sales for your business? Retrieved from https://blog.intellifluence.com/which-social-channel-will-bring-sales-for-your-business-c8831fb0c4e2

[83] Sinkwitz, J. (2016, October 18) Determining the right influencer type for your campaign. Retrieved from https://blog.intellifluence.com/determining-the-right-influencer-type-for-your-campaign-837a8fe94ff2

[84] Sinkwitz, J. (2016, October 26). Time to pick the right product influencers. Retrieved from https://blog.intellifluence.com/time-to-pick-the-right-product-influencers-531c13ed49a1

[85] Sinkwitz, J. (2016, October 31). How to pitch influencers. Retrieved from https://blog.intellifluence.com/how-to-pitch-influencers-5b2dd319a0c6

reviewer is diminished and a new reviewer is likely a better fit.

Unique with change. Based on the initial question, if the product is the same as used in the first wave of reviews, but changes have been made based on reviewer feedback, then it is overwhelmingly better to use the initial reviewers again. There's a strong positive psychological effect in letting someone know that not only did you value their feedback, but you also incorporated it. These follow-up reviews are almost always glowing, with influencers going out of their way to point out the product improvements and overlooking remaining flaws. Audiences that were exposed to the initial review and the follow-up review are also deeply influenced, perceiving the brand as more caring about its consumer base.

Habitual. The nature of this question is to determine if the product in question is one of constant use and purchase. For instance, most consumables such as cosmetics, food and drink, and other possible commodities wrapped into unique services like Uber or Airbnb are very habitual. The more habitual a product is in its use, the greater benefit there is in using the initial reviewers again. The less habitual, the better off you may be in selecting a new batch of reviewers for the second round.

Ideal audience. While you may have done your best to pick the product influencers with the information you had at hand, sometimes we discover more by undertaking a campaign. For the previous campaign, were you able to determine if the audience of the reviewer was ideal (that is, matched your buyer persona), regardless of whether or not they performed the action you wanted? If it was, message repetition may be useful in further reaching the audience. If the audience was not ideal, then the decision to use new reviewers is easier.

Repetition benefit. Is the buyer persona susceptible to advertising repetition per the compulsion marketing[86] concepts discussed in a previous chapter on maximizing exposure[87]? This point is covered somewhat in asking about habitual product use and ideal audience fit, but further, it seeks to answer a question for the product type rather than the product itself. Within your industry, is there a significant use of retargeting ads to continually remind potential consumers of specific brands relevant to products that can be purchased anywhere? I find e-commerce stores that aren't also the manufacturer of the products they sell fall into the category of benefiting from repetition benefit—in those cases, using the old reviewers has its benefit. This point is less true of very unique products where there are not many sellers or clear alternatives.

New discovery. From the last round to this round, time has passed and there may be other influencers available[88] for you to compare against the previous reviewer selections. Are

---

[86] Intellifluence (2016). Compulsion marketing: Making your campaign irresistible. Retrieved from https://www.slideshare.net/intellifluence/compulsion-marketing-making-your-campaign-irresistible

[87] Sinkwitz, J. (2016, December 7). How to maximize exposure on your product reviews. Retrieved from https://blog.intellifluence.com/how-to-maximize-exposure-on-your-product-reviews-23336c3492a4

[88] Intellifluence (2016). Find the right influencers and make more sales. Retrieved from https://intellifluence.com/discover?geo=all&network=all&category=all

any of these new influencers a better fit per the picking product reviewer article referenced above? If so, it may be a clear win to use new influencers.

CASE STUDY: FRANK BODY

Photo 13.2. Credit: Christopher Campbell

This mock case study would be for Sandra Kirwan of Frank Body. Note that Frank Body has done an incredible job using mid-level authoritative and strong influencers for their line to the point where they have been covered internationally for their success[89].

I have no knowledge of their plans, so here's a guess on how they would make a determination on using the same influencers or moving to fresh influencers.

Unique product? One of the products I see on Instagram is the original coffee scrub, the product that launched Frank Body. However, they have over 10 pretty unique products. Assuming the obvious success the first round of influence of the original coffee scrub had, if a different product is selected, using the same reviewers would score a point.

Unique with changes? This one I am uncertain on. It is entirely possible that product changes or perhaps packaging changes were made over the years—we'll skip this area.

Habitual? The cosmetics industry is such a great industry because if the product works, repurchases are high. Per our earlier notes, habitual products do benefit from repeat reviews. Another unrelated note for Frank Body would be to create a subscription service at a slight discount so a lazy person like me could get an order of coffee scrub on a monthly basis without needing to come back every month.

Ideal audience? Again, this one is very clear that for most of the Instagram influencers selected, the buyer personas were 100 percent and the audience is ideal, given the commercial success — another point for the repeat reviewers.

Repetition benefit? Cosmetics are constantly compared against each other for their efficacy; as such, it is the brand and product benefits that consumers need to be constantly reminded of as being a superior choice — a point for repeat reviewers.

New discovery? The likelihood of finding drastically better influencers is somewhat low, considering how well their initial campaigns have worked out. However, by mapping the audience of their existing influencers and comparing it against the possibility of using new influencers, they may find areas where some individuals matching their buyer persona have

---

[89] Garcia, A. (2015, November 7). How this company earns millions with Instagram. Retrieved from http://money.cnn.com/2015/11/07/smallbusiness/frank-body-startup-coffee-scrub/index.html

not yet been reached. At present, I would still say the point goes to a repeat reviewer, but I would not rule out discovery sourcing as a better fit.

A TWIST!

What if you didn't have to choose? The beauty of peer reviewing influencers is they tend to be far more affordable than other forms of marketing. As such, you don't necessarily have to choose using new over old reviewers or vice versa. As a twist, you could approach a new batch of product reviewers like you approached the last batch, while also reapproaching the old influencers with a different offer, such as money to repromote their old review with language on how they still use the product or mentioning product changes (such as "now in mint!"). You may be surprised at how effective and cost-favorable such repromotions are.

Photo 14.1. Credit: Pexels.com

CHAPTER 14

Post-Mortem: Why We Test

A post-mortem is a retrospective analysis on the goal, the process taken, and the conclusion. Learn the benefits of using post-mortems to tie back into one's goal setting and how to successfully perform a post-mortem step by step, as well as the types of questions to ask to ensure the next campaign yields even better results.

You have reached the end of the internet, otherwise known as Chapter 14, the final chapter specifically for brands. Appropriately, it seems like a good time to raise the subject of performing post-mortem analysis on your campaigns. Presumably to get to this point you started with a goal[90], picked a buyer persona[91] to target, decided on an influencer type[92] to match your preferred social network[93], identified the influencer[94] from that filtering, pitched[95] that influencer, maybe negotiated[96] a bit, and now you need to ask yourself the big question: How did it go?

---

[90] Sinkwitz, J. (2016, September 28). How to set goals for your influencer campaign. Retrieved from https://blog.intellifluence.com/how-to-set-goals-for-your-influencer-campaign-abc236257f79

[91] Sinkwitz, J. (2016, October 5). Who exactly are you trying to influence? Retrieved from https://blog.intellifluence.com/who-are-you-trying-to-influence-ba8ddaf5a575

[92] Sinkwitz, J. (2016, October 18). Determining the right influencer type for your campaign. Retrieved from https://blog.intellifluence.com/determining-the-right-influencer-type-for-your-campaign-837a8fe94ff2

[93] Sinkwitz, J. (2016, October 11). Which social channel will bring sales for your business? Retrieved from https://blog.intellifluence.com/which-social-channel-will-bring-sales-for-your-business-c8831fb0c4e2

[94] Sinkwitz, J. (2016, October 26). Time to pick the right product influencers. Retrieved from https://blog.intellifluence.com/time-to-pick-the-right-product-influencers-531c13ed49a1

[95] Sinkwitz, J. (2016, October 31). How to pitch influencers. Retrieved from https://blog.intellifluence.com/how-to-pitch-influencers-5b2dd319a0c6

[96] Sinkwitz, J. (2016, November 28). Influencer negotiation: What is fair? Retrieved from https://blog.intellifluence.com/influencer-negotiation-what-is-fair-20f05dac4234

WHAT IS A POST-MORTEM?

The medical definition of a post-mortem is the autopsy used to determine a cause of death. The marketing world's use of the phrase isn't quite as morbid; it is actually closer to military after-action reports, which are a retrospective analysis on the goal, the process taken, and the conclusion. The goal, in essence, is to determine why goals were or were not met.

HOW TO PERFORM A SUCCESSFUL POST-MORTEM

The following process can, and should be, performed after every marketing campaign. Testing and evaluating those tests are the best way to move from a novice to an intermediate and ultimately to an advanced practitioner. In some ways, this chapter could be the first post of this series because you must have an eye to the conclusion of a campaign at its onset.

Take notes. If you don't have notes on the overall process, you'll be going by memory and may miss some critical missteps like when IT took five days to set up a retargeting pixel and then finance extended your approval period to pay an influencer[97] $50 in addition to offering product, which resulted in the influencer assuming you weren't serious. It isn't about note taking for assigning blame; you need to have objective data points to discuss.

Team meeting. Include all the stakeholders on your campaign, not just marketing. Were there elements that involved the IT department or dev ops for deploying unique coupons and setting retargeting pixels? If someone was involved, include them, sending an email outline to the types of questions that need to be covered in order to focus on continual improvement of the entire campaign process.

Discuss the data. Share the data on what was spent, internal labor used, and the goal completion, plus any unexpected benefits. Keep emotions out of this process and do not assign blame. The important matter is to show timelines for the campaign, resources used, and the results. It isn't enough to focus just on revenue and expenses,

Photo 14.2. Credit: startupstockphotos.com

traffic, shares, or whatever your goal metric was. There could be other questions that arise from the data that merit discussion:

1. If your revenue goal was achieved but all the revenue came from existing customers, this finding might indicate that the influencer campaign was successful in engaging your base, but not so much for extending your audience reach.

2. If the revenue goal was overachieved, but returns also exceed expectations, this

97 Intellifluence (2016). Welcome, influencers. Retrieved from https://intellifluence.com/influencers

item might indicate customers responding to the psychological triggers, but not being the right buyers.

3. If traffic was fantastic, but the bounce rate was also very high, then the influencer may have been good at engaging the audience, but that audience wasn't a good fit—or the audience didn't perceive your product offering as being of sufficient value.

4. Did online sales mostly stay within expected averages, but phone or in-store traffic spiked? Pay attention to the indirect methods by which goals might be reached, in those unexpected spillovers.

5. How does the data compare with other industry campaigns you have data on?

Listen to other learnings. If other teams are undertaking their own form of post-mortem reporting, aggregate those reports and draw from them to find parallels to your campaign. This time is an opportunity to knowledge share and use that to identify organizational problems affecting more than just your campaign; addressing those problems will help all teams.

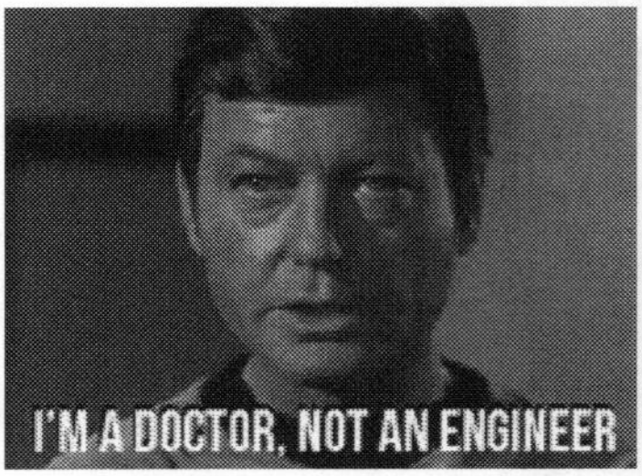

Stick to your agenda. It is vital that your agenda questions are adhered to and not go off-track. This meeting isn't the time to vent or turn into an HR meeting about why Jim in engineering doesn't pull his weight ... dammit Jim.

Here are some sample agenda questions to cover:

I'M A DOCTOR, NOT AN ENGINEER

Photo 14.3. Credit: startupstockphotos.com

Communication questions:

1. Were team members accessible when they needed to assist?

2. Was there any confusion or difficulty on building team consensus?

3. Was the goal[99] set understood by everyone on the team?

4. How much time was spent on meetings? Were they necessary?

5. Was individual expertise respected or was it drowned out by preconceived notions?

6. Were stakeholders made aware of progress, or lack thereof, throughout the campaign?

Process questions:

1. Why was the deadline date what it was?

2. Was there clear prioritization of tasks?

[99] Sinkwitz, J. (2016, September 28). How to set goals for your influencer campaign. Retrieved from https://blog.intellifluence.com/how-to-set-goals-for-your-influencer-campaign-abc236257f79

3. Was there appropriate coordination of those tasks to ensure prioritization was preserved?

4. Were the task timeline estimates accurate?

5. What roadblocks existed that were not identified prior to kickoff?

Role questions:

1. Were the team roles clear as a function of the task prioritization above?

2. Was it necessary to involve external parties as key role players? [Since this question is on influencer marketing, that would be a yes—so the real question becomes how those external parties worked in concert with the team.]

3. Who had the decision-making authority for the project?

4. Was the decision maker responsible for ensuring all tasks were appropriately assigned?

Future questions (that is, why we're bothering to go through this sometimes painful process):

1. Should any of the roles change for future iterations based on the outcome?

2. Should the existing process be modified for a faster turnaround, a lowered expense, or a greater revenue achievement?

3. Does management need to play a different role in overseeing the project to keep peer-level team members focused?

4. Should any additional process items be added for amplification purposes [99]?

Remember, the post-mortem won't work if it isn't taken seriously and the agenda followed. Even if you manage to make seemingly minor process improvements, the outsized outcome as you scale on influencer marketing could be enormous. If you manage to learn from both your failures and successes, you'll be that much better on your next campaign[100].

As you can see, influencer marketing can be applied to enterprise international megacorps and local small businesses alike, both those that sell to C-level executives and to neighborhood grandmothers. If you apply the lessons learned from this guide, it is my hope that you'll have all the success I believe you can have.

In the next half of this book, we'll cover everything an individual needs to know to become a top-tier influencer.

---

[99] Sinkwitz, J. (2016, December 7). How to maximize exposure on your product reviews. Retrieved from https://blog.intellifluence.com/how-to-maximize-exposure-on-your-product-reviews-23336c3492a4

[100] Sinkwitz, J. (2016, December 14). Round two: Use the same reviewers or get new ones? Retrieved from https://blog.intellifluence.com/round-two-use-the-same-reviewers-or-get-new-ones-8cc22e349bd0

PART 2

The Ultimate Guide to Becoming a Top-Tier Influencer

Prologue

What I've written over the past several months is what I hope you'll find to be a detailed guide on how to become what you might consider a top-tier influencer and is meant to be the continuation of the first part of this book: the Ultimate Guide to Using Influencer Marketing[101]. The process is designed to start with understanding visibility, picking a focus on where you have the most capacity to influence, learning how to expand on that capacity, learning a variety of tactics and concepts for audience growth, and along the way, perhaps transforming your life in a positive manner.

Before you embark on what I hope is a whirlwind of success becoming the next big thing in...whatever it is that interests you, I want to provide some advice that transcends the rest of the series.

1. **Disclose.** Proper disclosure is very important and can keep you out of trouble. According to our research, adding #ad as a minimal disclosure on tweets, Facebook, Instagram, YouTube, and Instagram posts doesn't even impact the bottom line. However, it can keep you from being targeted with fines for not following the rules. When in doubt, disclose.

2. **Honesty.** If you're offered money and asked to review a product or service in a way that isn't in line with reality, turn it down. This point goes along with proper disclosure because you are attaching your name

---

[101] Sinkwitz, J. (2017, January 5). The ultimate guide to using influencer marketing. Retrieved by https://blog.intellifluence.com/the-ultimate-guide-to-using-influencer-marketing-69021bae4b06

to the review. There are still ways to provide an honest review without slamming a product or service by focusing on attributes that you do like, but don't lie. Think about how you'd feel if you bought the product based on someone else's review only to find out it wasn't any good, and then keep that feeling in mind as you review.

3. **Have fun.** This offering is an opportunity to be paid for playing around in an area that interests you, so don't forget to let yourself enjoy the experience. If by the end of the process you say, "I actually get paid to do this," then I'll have done my job.

Are you ready? I won't use the cliché of "Kid, I'm going to make you a star," but I would be very happy if that was the outcome.

Photo 15.1. Credit: Blubel.

CHAPTER 15

Becoming a Top-Tier Influencer: Get Visible

Get an understanding on the importance of visibility as it pertains to the influencer's journey, which includes a primer on how visibility works on Amazon, blogs, Facebook, Instagram, LinkedIn, Pinterest, Twitter, and YouTube. Finally, explore a teaser on engagement and the importance of interlinking social profiles.

Welcome to Chapter 15, now let's help you become the best possible influencer. If you are actually looking to use influencer marketing, we published a massive guide[102] on the subject in Part 1 of this book. If you're looking to grow as an influencer, you're in the right place. This discussion is going to focus on visibility. If you aren't visible, no one will know you exist, and your influence reach won't be as far and wide as it obviously could be.

BUILD IN THE WRONG PLACE AND THEY WON'T COME

It should be intuitive that if you are trying to make a name for yourself and are spending the majority of your time doing so in a low-traffic area, or in the wrong section on even the right social network, chances are your growth is going to be anemic. The "build and they'll come" philosophy only works if you're building your presence in an area with a lot of existing traffic. A hot dog vendor on a busy Manhattan street is going to do a lot more business than a cart of the same quality in the middle of a deserted highway.

ALWAYS BE BROADCASTING

There's no way to get around this unless you're a massive celebrity. To build up an audience and keep them following you, you need to always be thinking about what you're going to share, when you're going to share it, and how you're going to go about post-production engagement. Salesmen need to always be closing. Educators need to always be teaching; influencers need to always be broadcasting.

OBVIOUS AND NON-OBVIOUS PLACES TO BUILD VISIBILITY

Non-obvious placement first. I just spent some keyboard time telling you that you shouldn't place a hot dog cart in the middle of a deserted highway. However, being the only hot dog cart downtown in a bustling small city can sometimes yield better results than being one of 100 hot dog carts in a single block in Manhattan. The analogy is used to describe the importance of niche communities. What do I mean with niche communities?

- If you're a top-tier e-commerce professional, chances are you are hanging out with Jeremy of mommymakeup.com on Ecommercefuel.com. Of course, it will be less overall traffic than that of Twitter, but the focus and self-selection is strong to where if you intended to become an e-commerce influencer, you need to be here.

- If you're a crusty old webmaster, chances are you have an account at webmasterworld. Affiliate marketer? You might hang out on BHW or BuilderSociety.

- Etc., etc., etc. Niche communities of a good size are a very good place to learn and establish yourself, which you can then use for audience expansion on the more obvious places.

---

[102] Sinkwitz, J. (2017, January 5). The ultimate guide to using influencer marketing. Retrieved by https://blog.intellifluence.com/the-ultimate-guide-to-using-influencer-marketing-69021bae4b06

For those obvious places, as of this writing, Intellifluence supports the following network filters when matchmaking brands and filters: Amazon, blogs, Facebook, Instagram, LinkedIn, Pinterest, Twitter, and YouTube. Now, keep in mind that we are network agnostic, meaning that matchmaking does occur for other networks within the system, but this area is just our focus. Let's dig into each of these networks:

Amazon. Amazon isn't a typical social network in that you won't find a lot of reviewer interaction outside of heavily commented product threads and in the reviewer support forum. However, brands won't know about a reviewer unless they can FIND an influencer, which means leaving a high volume of quality product reviews. Let's get something out of the way: Amazon is cracking down on incentivized reviews, but there's still value in having an active profile, because Amazon's meteoric rise as a product search engine means some Amazon sellers are using it as a means to find influencers for other networks as well. I wrote a bit about how that works here[103].

Blogs. Blogs are going to be the most varied discovery mechanism, if only because there's no one standard way to blog. That said, there are a few considerations if you want to build visibility through blogging:

1. Write for your publication often. Need to improve as a copywriter? CopyPress has a guide for that[104].

2. Write for other publications as much as you can. Tiffany Sun has some good tips on how to get better at this.

3. We'll cover it more in a later chapter, but comment engagement is key.

Facebook. Facebook is huge. Now that we got that out of the way, you need to know that there's a difference between fan pages and personal profiles, which make life difficult for networks. If you're intending to grow your visibility primarily on Facebook, you'll want to get a fan page and do the majority of your interaction through this profile, because it is easier for brands and networks to track your activity .... It's a privacy issue and alleviates the follower cap problem associated with hard limits on personal friend network size. Other Facebook tips?

1. Join as many relevant groups as you can and stay active in them. Post and comment on other's posts: Like and share content, and you'll find your content getting liked and shared in return.

2. Go live! Until it is ubiquitous, Facebook is algorithmically preferring going live, which means if you have an idea for a quick live video, this idea is a fantastic way to stay

[103] Sinkwitz, J. (2016, October 3). Amazon: No more incentivized reviews". Retrieved from https://blog.intellifluence.com/amazon-no-more-incentivized-reviews-d109ad66ad64

[104] CopyPress (n.d.). Copywriting guide. Retrieved from http://community.copypress.com/guides/copywriting/the-basics/why-do-people-share-online-content/

top of mind and improve the probability of getting shared to a broader audience. A caveat though is to not abuse this format. Going live with videos that nobody wants is a quick way to losing followers and digital friends.

Instagram. Instagram is currently our most popular network for a few reasons. It is very easy to use; imagery has a high consumption rate, and e-commerce brands in the fields of fashion, cosmetics, health, etc. can't get enough influencers to satisfy demand. Growing visibility here is easy:

Photo 15.2. Credit: Jeremy Levin.

It's all about the hashtags. Unlike Twitter and its 140-character limitations, Instagram's larger limit means you can use significantly more hashtags on your content. This use comes into play in three ways:

1. You should be following as many relevant tag searches as you can to get a better sense of what is popular for your interests. Leave relevant comments and like as much as you can without being perceived as a thirsty spammer. Follow as many of those posters as you can. (There are daily limits, so be aware that getting too aggressive might earn you a temporary suspension.)

2. Produce as many high-quality posts as you can, using those same relevant tags. Interact with the comments left on your posts.

3. Shout out to slightly bigger and slightly smaller accounts. Shoutouts are the closest thing to sharing Instagram has at the moment. You can shout out to whatever content you wish, but peer psychology effects will be greater if you're of a similar size...it'll help you grow faster.

LinkedIn. LinkedIn doesn't get nearly as much love as it should. Not only is it a great place to build an audience, but by building up your professional presence, you're almost certainly going to improve your career prospects. What should you do?

1. Add all your existing professional contacts. This point should go without saying.

2. View profiles of your professional peers. We're all egoists on some level, and people like knowing their profiles were special enough to be viewed. A certain percentage of those people will friend you. Unless the account is spam, accept it. Most people don't share frequent updates on LinkedIn, so there'll be less pressure to constantly share. This network isn't Facebook after all (sorry, pet peeve).

3. Write articles for LinkedIn Pulse. LinkedIn no longer accepts applications to become

an influencer, but Pulse is the next best thing because the posts are very easy to share within the LinkedIn ecosystem, and thus become network expanding. If you do get a big enough following, it is still possible to become an influencer ... just not easy.

4. LinkedIn groups are a thing. While the activity is barely an echo of what occurs on Facebook groups for comparable subjects, some can be gold, with members directly friending each other. It can be a hidden gold mine to vastly increase your network size.

Pinterest. Similar to Instagram, Pinterest's focus is on very visual elements. The main difference is user focus. Our contention is that Pinterest is for saving imagery more for personal use, internally focused, whereas Instagram's default nature is to share with the world. The overlap is significant and some of the brands focusing on Pinterest (primarily food and fashion) are doing quite well, but don't write it off as a niche-only female-centric network. It is far more diverse. Ramya Menon has some great tips for this. To paraphrase:

1. Curate your actionable content from your blog (if you have one). Appropriately name it for SEO purposes: pinboard name, recipe name, full description.

2. Join as many relevant boards as possible

3. Create looooooong pins — don't just drop an image in a pin and move on. Load it up like a mini-blog post.

4. Follow relevant pinners and boards, engage with them, and you'll receive the same in kind.

Photo 15.3. Credit: Freestocks.org

Twitter. Want to reach as many people as possible the quickest? Twitter is still king for this item. It is the social network that skews more toward topic and interest than friend network. In this manner, if you're able to latch on to a trending topic, the potential for building a network fast is incredible. Just ask Ken Bone who went from pretty much nothing to 237K in a week or so—had controversy not cropped up, who knows how big his audience might have gotten? How can you increase your visibility on Twitter?

1. Hashtags are even more important than on Instagram. Due to message size constraints, one is forced to use only the most relevant hashtags, so tag use tends to be a bit more focused. Like, follow, and retweet as much relevant content as you want initially from the core tag searches you identify.

2. Once you have a little bit of an audience, start producing your own thought-provoking tweets. Quote tweets also count for this approach — their use has shifted from providing commentary to more public commenting in a new thread. Keep using relevant hashtags in this comment and you'll start to build up a following to those passionate about the subject.

3. Partake in Twitter chats. On a daily basis, there always seems to be a focused Q&A chat occurring. If such chats exist for your core focus, partake in them as you would in your hashtag co-opting, and your audience should continue to grow as the best answers end up getting retweeted and featured in blog recap articles.

YouTube. YouTube can be the trickiest network because the time component of content production is the steepest. If you have a great camera presence, YouTube might be right for you. Assuming you know how to create a channel and upload videos, how do you go about increasing your visibility here?

1. Comment on relevant videos. The YouTube community is fragmented into producers and non-producers. If you're leaving thoughtful and intelligent comments on videos related to your subject material, you're going to draw attention, which is important for later.

2. Quality matters. The beauty of Twitter is the time required to push out 140 characters and have it be useful is minimal. If you're a makeup vlogger, though, you have to put time and thought into setting up the concept, script, production, and post-production. Quality videos are very much appreciated though, leading to subscribers.

3. Collab. Leading into the next segment of the article, collaboration is massive on YouTube. The ability to engage with other influencers in the creative process is very synergistic and is how a lot of the major channels keep growth constant. When you're new, start by producing reaction videos. As you pick up an audience, you can then pitch other creators on ideas for collaborations.

ENGAGE

The more you engage with other influencers, in a collaborative and supportive fashion, the more likely you are to have success. When I'm writing material relevant to influencer marketing, I want someone like Lee Odden seeing it, due to his role

Graphic 15.4. Source: Allergic Reputation on DeviantArt

in the industry. Likewise, interacting in a positive manner with his material increases the likelihood of success. The group success improves individual success, and thus the incentive for altruism exists.

INTERLINK TO RULE THEM ALL

It's very difficult to be a top-tier influencer on every single major social channel, yet alone all social channels. However, it is possible to maintain a presence on all the major channels, the goal being to push the audience toward your preferred channel. If you want to be top tier on YouTube, there is nothing wrong with reposting videos on Instagram, embed posting on Facebook, and sharing the video on Twitter — so long as you are genuinely active on the other channels, you can use them as capillaries to funnel traffic to where you want attention the most.

The same can be even said of bloggers. When I post a blog, I'll end up reposting on LinkedIn Pulse, in Quora, Reddit, Inbound, Growthhackers, maybe a Slack channel or two, and will share on Twitter and Facebook. If I don't remain active in any of those channels, the efforts will be meaningless, but by being active, I can ensure that attention is drawn and the channels will help to improve the audience where I want it most. You can do the same.

Photo 16.1 Credit: Stokpic

CHAPTER 16

Becoming a Top-Tier Influencer: Focus and Authenticity

After visibility is understood, the most critical step is to select a focus and remain committed to that focus. Learn how to cultivate your persona and utilize various tools to source content which can help you to get started in that niche. The goal is to work toward expertise.

In our previous chapter, we discussed the importance of being visible[105] for those wanting to maximize their influence. The next logical step, after knowing where to focus, is determining what to focus on. In our opinion, the best path forward — if you're not already a mega celebrity — is to focus on a niche and remain authentic in your postings within that niche.

Taken further, Nic Haralambous suggests that with regards to one's focus, it is a matter of playing a specific niche rather than appealing to the entire population. In his article[106], he provides the analogy of wearing a very colorful scarf and how that experience helped him understand that trying to please the masses is very different than doing something specific that you know will definitely make your target audience happy.

BE SELECTIVE

One way to ensure you are perceived as being authentic to that niche audience is to be selective with your reviews. The short-term monies gained by reviewing all products pitched to you are easily surpassed by remaining true to your focus and being sought after as a true niche player. Adelyn Zhou of Greylock has a great piece on influencer marketing mastery. I reference it here[107] because a lack of focus will result in low engagement, and that's one of the major red flags to look out for by brands seeking influencers. Let's avoid that!

Referencing Oleksiy Kuryliak, we see why there's another very good reason you should focus primarily on your chosen niche: In his case study, it was determined that focused content results in greater time on the page and more overall traffic, as niche material has a greater share rate and a deeper spread within niche communities. Not only are traffic and on-page positive engagement signals for you and your own monetization, but they also tend to bleed into other signals that brands look for: shares, likes, and comments.

By focusing and being selective, you are making yourself a more attractive choice to brands.

FOLLOW YOUR DREAMS: BUILD A PERSONA

Cliché alert: Following ones' dreams is only meant to point out that everyone has hobbies and dream-like interests.

Graphic 16.1.

[105] Sinkwitz, J. (2017, Jan. 17). Become a top-tier influencer. Retrieved from https://blog.intellifluence.com/becoming-a-top-tier-influencer-get-visible-c8286796392e

[106] Haralambous, N. (2016, July 1). Find a niche, not a population. Retrieved from https://medium.com/found-it/find-a-niche-not-a-population-2a588bfe39f6

[107] Zhou, A. (2016, May 16). Mastering influencer marketing: 9 key questions and answers. Retrieved from https://news.greylock.com/how-to-master-influencer-marketing-9-key-questions-and-answers-c14ff728d6a5

By zeroing in on those interests for the majority of content creation, the authentic nature of those product reviews will shine through.

Too vague? We can build a persona. Let's say by day you're a mom, a wife, an actuarial accountant, or someone who likes drinking coffee and reading on the couch during the 10 minutes of downtime you have every other Saturday morning when the kids are still in a cereal-induced coma on the couch. You've also been known to sing karaoke in the car, can squat two plates, and are passionate about pomegranate smoothies.

In the above persona, where should the focus be? It's entirely up to you of course, but fitness and nutrition would stand out, perhaps with an analytical twist from your accounting background that allows you to stand apart from the other fitness and nutrition bloggers and influencers. If I were in a marketing meeting with you, I'd pitch concepts like "Mom Fit: By the Numbers."

If this idea sounds somewhat formulaic and scientific, we actually recommend that brands perform similar exercises[108] to build buyer personas[109]. By working in reverse on those guidelines, you can see how focused you may appear in ticking off the checkboxes. A brand that is searching for influencers matching a buyer persona that appears to be a mother interested in fitness is going to be very interested in having someone like you reviewing its product. This point is especially true if the product requires an analytical mind to understand.

HOW DO I FOCUS ON MY FOCUS?

Sometimes, after settling on a select few niches, it is easy to become overwhelmed, not knowing where to start. Sean Ogle compiled a fantastic post on 59 tools[110] to assist in sourcing and creating content, which you can use as a guide for finding content that is already working in your niche so you can apply your own spin …. "Mom Fit: By the Numbers," remember? It's also a great way to find who the perceived experts are in your space, which is even more important as you attempt to become an expert.

Once you have determined the experts in your space, clarifying your message will help you stand out, cut through a lot of the competing noise, and connect with the right audience. You already have your focus. You know the experts. Now it's time to develop your own strategy to differentiate yourself from these other experts in order to tell your story in a unique way that will capture the attention of your audience.

Building on the aforementioned example, perhaps there are many other influential fitness and nutrition mom experts in your space. Figure out ways you can attract attention. Maybe

[108] Sinkwitz, J. (2016, September 19). Why should influencer marketing be a part of your strategy? Retrieved from https://blog.intellifluence.com/why-should-influencer-marketing-be-a-part-of-your-strategy-88122ece9dab

[109] Sinkwitz, J. (2016, October 5). Who exactly are you trying to influence? Retrieved from https://blog.intellifluence.com/who-are-you-trying-to-influence-ba8ddaf5a575

[110] Ogle, S. (2016, September 13) 59 amazing tools to help you create remarkable content easily. Retrieved from https://medium.com/@seanogle/59-amazing-tools-to-help-you-create-remarkable-content-easily-f406f0ae3c99

you have a particular fashion sense you can bring into the mix. Maybe you have a certain nutritional philosophy you could promote. A unique, consistent message will help you engage the best followers in your niche.

NOTHING MORE AUTHENTIC THAN AN EXPERT

Becoming a topical expert is the best way to maximize authenticity. From an influence perspective, it is known as authoritative influence[111], and it is very powerful because it is the next step from a casual

Photo 16.2 Credit: freestocks.org

product reviewer applying peer influence. Authorities generally have a greater topical reach (meaning your audience is likely to increase) and are trusted especially when taking an educational and informational tone. Authorities are sought after for commerce reasons.

Becoming an expert is hard work. There aren't any shortcuts as Mike Koenigs explains in his how to[112] for becoming an expert for the purposes of writing a book. I like his guide because it provides a useful parallel—there isn't too much of a difference between a blogger that is hyperactive on social media and a book author. Being perceived as an expert isn't a particularly complex concept, but it is very time consuming. If you were to conduct and publish interviews with all the other experts in your niche, you will start to become an expert in your own right, both in real terms due to the sheer amount of time put in and also via co-citation perception. Your name appearing alongside other experts repeatedly will cause readers in the niche to see you as an expert.

PUT INTO PRACTICE

At this point, after the first two chapters in this part of the book, you should have enough information to accurately fill out an influencer profile at a network. Often, I'm contacted by influencers asking why it isn't sufficient to just list their Twitter, Instagram, or YouTube profile. Selecting the right categories and creating a profile that reads like a buyer persona is key and will result in more pitches consisting of the opportunities you want to see.

[111] Sinkwitz, I. (2016, October 18). Determining the right influencer type for your campaign. Retrieved from https://blog.intellifluence.com/determining-the-right-influencer-type-for-your-campaign-837a8fe94ff2

[112] Koenigs, M. (2016, June 23). How to find your niche (for your business or your book). Retrieved from https://medium.com/@MikeKoenigs/how-to-find-your-niche-for-your-business-or-your-book-f22db3104c79

Photo 17.1 Credit: Cosmic Timetraveler

CHAPTER 17

Optimize Your Influence

Grasp the importance of optimizing for one's niche and how it pertains to content marketing and SEO. Then, explore an in-depth look at how to specifically source and utilize trends and content discovery on Facebook, LinkedIn, Twitter, Instagram, Pinterest, and YouTube for the purposes of crafting an optimization strategy for your persona. An example persona chosen for this primer is that of a cosmetics blogger.

Before you can attempt to optimize your influence online, make sure that you first understand where you want to be visible[113] and what your main focus[114] will be. The analogy I like to use here is attempting to pick out the perfect pair of shoes without first understanding what activity and what occasion the shoes are for. OK: I know nothing about shoes, but I'm pretty sure buying Italian loafers for a marathon isn't a great idea.

WHY OPTIMIZE?

Maximizing your influence isn't just about trying to get discovered for high-value phrases such as fashion or cosmetics —vanity phrases are great, just like in SEO, but as you can see in this article[115] by Catalin Zorzini, just like in SEO, there's a lot more to it. If you want my opinion on his comparison, Ahrefs + SpyFu is a great combination. I personally use them for my marketing projects and would suggest that, when doing keyword research, you should as well.

If you optimize your organic content to trending topics within your niche and subsection focus, you will appear more authentic than someone who is reviewing everything and anything related to fashion or all cosmetics.

HOW TO OPTIMIZE, BY NETWORK

It is a lot easier to simply tell an influencer[116] to hyper focus than it is to explain how, so let's explain how, making the assumption that you're a somewhat new cosmetics blogging influencer. The how to isn't just about how to go viral[117], though following some of the advice from Austin Iuliano will certainly help to boost your overall visibility.

FACEBOOK

Let's start with Anne DiVitto's piece on four ways to use Facebook trending. One method in Facebook trending[118] would be to hashtagjack, meaning to find a trending topic that you could possibly weigh in on related to your niche and use the trending hashtag. Using this tactic, your message will be exposed to many more people that are actively consuming that specific trending news. Another more nuanced method involves searching on the vanity hashtag phrase first, such as #cosmetics, and exploring the other tags commonly used in conjunction with that main phrase. Since in this example you are a newish cosmetics blogger, #beautyblogger may be even more relevant. Do you have a dedicated blog for this

[113] Sinkwitz, J. (2017, January 17). Becoming a top-tier influencer. Get visible. Retrieved from https://blog.intellifluence.com/becoming-a-top-tier-influencer-get-visible-c8286796392e

[114] Sinkwitz, J. (2017, January 26). Becoming a top-tier influencer: Focus and authenticity. Retrieved from https://blog.intellifluence.com/becoming-a-top-tier-influencer-focus-and-authenticity-91b2ec154d0e

[115] Zorzini, C. (2016, October 24). SemRush vs Ahrefs vs SpyFu vs Majestic vs Moz. Retrieved from https://medium.com/@zorzini/semrush-vs-ahrefs-vs-spyfu-vs-majestic-vs-moz-ddc035b53dda

[116] Intellifluence (2016). Welcome, influencers. Retrieved from https://intellifluence.com/influencers

[117] Iuliano, A. (2016, October 29). How to go viral on every social media. Retrieved from https://medium.com/@AustinIuliano/how-to-go-viral-on-every-social-media-9ed589379ec8

[118] DiVitto, A. (2016, September 11). 4 ways to use Facebook trending topics for your business. Retrieved from https://blog.markgrowth.com/4-ways-to-use-facebook-trending-topics-for-your-business-6086d63e9559

one? Alternatively, #beautyblog and other variations make sense to focus on for optimized discovery purposes.

LINKEDIN

There was a recent post on LinkedIn Pulse[119] by Larry Kim, which was once a great method to maximize spread on LinkedIn Pulse. LinkedIn recently made some changes, though, so now content posting is more about enticing people to follow and friend you. All of Larry's advice for titles and imagery apply here. Additionally, if you are looking to hyper focus, use another network like Facebook or Twitter to first determine the more focused hashtags that are in use, then create pieces surrounding those phrases to highlight on your personal profile and search for those phrases, adding professional connections that closely match those searches. Since you are going to appear more relevant with content that matches their profiles, the acceptance ratio will be higher.

Photo 17.2 Credit: kaboompics.com

TWITTER

It is in vogue to hate on Twitter lately. Some, such as Scott Kleinberg with his piece on the disappointment of Twitter Moments[120], is justified. In it, he shows that Twitter Moments could have been significantly more powerful than Facebook's trending feature if implemented corrected. Even as a somewhat broken product though, there is significant value in hashtag jacking through the same mechanism. As I write this chapter, one of the trending stories is on "The Bachelor fans are in love with Rachel." It would be fairly easy to tweet in those moments and put on a cosmetics spin to make the content appear relevant and turn it into a new moment as well. The moments jacking concept is an underused method, but another can bring you further optimized focus. Twitter offers a more searchable trending than Facebook at https://twitter.com/search-home. The top trends show, but if you were to search for cosmetics, many top and latest tweets show with a multitude of fantastic hashtags for you to start using that might be more specific to your focus. Since Twitter is constrained to 140 characters, users have to be judicious in which tags to use, so the niche tags you see are more likely to be useful.

INSTAGRAM

Want to get nerdy with me? The Instagram Engineering team shared how trending works on Instagram[121]. It's the technical methodology behind how trends are sourced. I absolutely love that stuff, but ... too much math? OK. Finding a trend to attach yourself to on Instagram

[119] Kim, L. (2017, January 19). 11 ways to hack the LinkedIn Pulse algorithm. Retrieved from https://medium.com/marketing-and-entrepreneurship/11-ways-to-hack-the-linkedin-pulse-algorithm-219813bf8b7b

[120] Kleinberg, S. (2015, November 5). Twitter moments: There's no lightning. Retrieved from https://medium.com/@scottkleinberg/twitter-moments-there-s-no-lightning-6fbb786d9fe6

[121] Instagram Engineering (2015, July 6). Trending on Instagram. Retrieved from https://engineering.instagram.com/trending-on-instagram-b749450e6d93?gi=2de0f8d676d0

is like a cross between Twitter and Facebook. On the search feature, you'll notice that live videos are given preference—keep this point in mind as you are building content here, as both Facebook and Instagram are overweighting algorithmically toward "live" content. In that search feature, if you search for cosmetics, you'll see a mix of tags and accounts to follow, but if you select tags, everything will become clear, where tags even have post statistics to help you make your choices. This information may seem a lot like Twitter, but where the Facebook likeness comes in is that you'll need to follow and comment and use those chosen tags as described in our first chapter on the series governing visibility. Also like Facebook, the message sizes aren't as limiting, so more hashtags can be used for message spread.

PINTEREST

If there ever was a network for you, my new cosmetics blogger, it is Pinterest. It doesn't take long to find posts like this one[122] by Tony Yeung that highlight the types of material that trends on Pinterest within the fashion and beauty niches. Pinterest goes so far as to even provide fantastic trend predictions for its users. Since you're in beauty, look at pages 11–20; as you can see, it is slightly different than Twitter-type trends where the trends are extremely focused. I won't pretend to understand what jojoba oil and ash balayage are, but if you are able to break into these subset niches by producing content around them, you could use that sourced material up elsewhere on Twitter, where hashtags are at a premium, to become an optimized expert. For those of us not in cosmetics or fashion, there's of course a lot more happening on Pinterest to help you source popular material the way Twitter Moments should probably work. Of course, it still skews toward fashion, cosmetics, fitness, and food and drink, but if you're in those niches, it provides for massive exposure that can be optimized.

YOUTUBE

YouTube is kind enough to provide trending searches for finding trending videos, which, for the most part, are likely to be as relevant as Twitter Moments. If you can quickly produce material related to these videos that matches your niche, you can garner some attention, but a better method is to simply perform a search for the main phrase (or optimized phrases if you already have them). Videos are ranked by a mix of what's recent and engagement — likes, subscribes, and comments, so the best material is right in front of you. Trolling through the top five videos in cosmetics, not only do I realize I'm woefully unaware of how products are supposed to be used in conjunction with each other, but I can also see that the better videos take extra effort to provide additional details in the show notes and provide descriptive titles. Similar to Instagram, you'll want to use similar language and terms in order to be able to show, but unlike Instagram, there's really no reason to use hashtags.

[122] Yeung, T. (2016, December 16). 7 popular fashion contests of this week. Pinterest marketing showcase. Retrieved from https://medium.com/@tkwyoung/7-popular-fashion-contents-of-this-week-pinterest-marketing-showcase-7e6c4f34af10

KEEP OPTIMIZING AND STAY FOCUSED

Typing back to the initial plea of hyper focusing, the above should help you understand how to go about optimizing for specific content, beyond the spray and pray that I see occurring in the cosmetics and fashion industry among newer influencers[123]. If you can really focus and show yourself as an expert on a sub niche, you can make a name for yourself, and with that showing will come the opportunities and money you deserve.

[123] Intellifluence (2016). Create an influencer account. Retrieved from https://intellifluence.com/influencers/register

Photo 18.1 Credit: Evan Clark

CHAPTER 18

Influencers Should Negotiate, Too

Should you accept every pitch? Should you negotiate? Why, when, and what for? Learn the importance on negotiating for fit as it pertains to niche optimization and when the lure of money should override that fit using the Take It? (TI) calculation. The assumptive examples for the calculations come from the skin care industry.

At this point in the process, if you're reading a piece on negotiating as an influencer, you have hopefully settled on an area of focus[124] and are working hard on constantly optimizing[125] your visibility[126]. If you are, then it is no surprise that you're now getting pitched[127]. The questions then are when and how should you negotiate.

In all fairness, we've written about negotiation[128] before, from the optics of a brand reaching out to an influencer. For the sake of not wasting word count, I'd like to only address a few critical pieces to that when it comes to the mechanics of negotiating.

1. Early on, you are best off establishing a relational negotiation strategy. Focus on a positive outcome for both parties that goes beyond immediate monetary needs—if the transaction is a success, the probability of a repeat opportunity is high.

2. Seek to understand what a satisfactory outcome for the brand is. Is its goal sales-based? Is it a play for more exposure? What kind of ROI is needed that would result in follow-up work for yourself?

3. After the reviews are in, seek feedback. Strange as it may be, some brands won't automatically tell you if something went wrong or if something went really right; you need to ask.

NEGOTIATE FOR FIT

If you've read the previous articles referenced above, you'll see that one of the themes I constantly try to hammer home is that of focus. This theme, then, probably won't shock you. Negotiate for fit over money initially, until you establish yourself as an expert. The money will absolutely come the more you are perceived as being authentic and authoritative to a niche.

Example: A newbie blogger who reviews everything for $50 vs. a newbie blogger who only focuses on her niche, taking free product and cash if offered so that she can work up the chain to larger opportunities in that niche. The blogger who takes all reviews will likely never rise much in terms of desire by brands—the focus is too fractured and rarely seen as a fit. If anything, the products to be reviewed will remain of a lower quality because the blogger will be seen as just another number ... another blog link ... another tweet ... another video. The other newbie blogger, however, may be limiting potential income initially, but by focusing on fit, will become more attractive to brands seeking fit in that niche.

[124] Sinkwitz, J. (2017, January 26). Becoming a top-tier influencer: Focus and authenticity. Retrieved from https://blog.intellifluence.com/becoming-a-top-tier-influencer-focus-and-authenticity-91b2ec154d0e
[125] Sinkwitz, J. (2017, February 1). Optimize your influence. Retrieved from https://blog.intellifluence.com/optimize-your-influence-6720367fce0e
[126] Sinkwitz, J. (2017, January 17). Becoming a top-tier influencer: Get visible. Retrieved from https://blog.intellifluence.com/becoming-a-top-tier-influencer-get-visible-c8286796392e
[127] Sinkwitz, J. (2016, October 31). How to pitch influencers. Retrieved from https://blog.intellifluence.com/how-to-pitch-influencers-5b2dd319a0c6
[128] Sinkwitz, J. (2016, November 28). Influencer negotiation: what is fair? Retrieved from https://blog.intellifluence.com/influencer-negotiation-what-is-fair-20f05dac4234

How important is that fit? According to Boostinsider, the fit[129] is everything. If you read closely, you'll see that the product-influencer fit is so important that monetary considerations become an afterthought. Think about it this way: Having the right influencer promoting the product is so important that it changes the perceived ROI calculation ... if you can build your presence to be seen as such an influencer, the money will come.

WHEN SHOULD YOU NEGOTIATE FOR MONEY?

When should you shift from negotiating for fit to money? Easy answer: when you are getting pitched mostly for your fit already and can become more selective. A takeaway to consider from Tandem in its piece on influence[130] is this: The chief problem of influencer marketing isn't its effectiveness, which by now is beyond repute, but rather the difficulty of scaling influencers due to the overriding importance of finding the ideal influencer-campaign fit, which, of course, goes back to understanding and focusing on buyer personas[131]. There isn't a magical industry calculation used in secret by the other 200 CEOs of influencer marketing companies as we sit around a very large table trying to determine how much each influencer is worth. I like math, though, so I came up with a simple formula you can use when deciding when you should shift from primarily considering fit to primarily considering money. Behold, the Take It? calculation:

TAKE IT? (TI) CALCULATION

(Value * Fit)/Market Rate = fit adjusted value of the opportunity

Value. The value in this calculation is the combined worth of the monetary and product considerations offered to you. A $50 offering that includes $25 of product would have a value of $75. Keep in mind that product worth is entirely dependent on you: The $25 worth of skin cream isn't going to be worth more than 25 cents to me, because I don't use it, but it might well be worth the full $25 to you.

Fit. This variable is easier to determine the more focused you intend to be. If you want to be known as the expert skin care influencer, then the skin cream offer above might be a 100 percent fit, expressed as a percentage (1). If you are a hair and beauty blogger, maybe it isn't perfect but still relevant, listed at (0.75) for a 75 percent fit. If you're me, then maybe (0.01), leaving the 1 percent chance I might find a use for it.

Market Rate. How do you determine market rate? In a Buffer piece on influencer marketing[132], which I think is a good complement to our own Ultimate Guide to Using

[129] Boostinsider (2016, October 21). What is product influencer fit? Retrieved from https://blog.boostinsider.com/what-is-product-influencer-fit-c2ef51d19b36?gi=a439db32dd12

[130] Tandem (2016, April 6). Marketing under the influence: Social media superstars as a marketing channel. Retrieved from https://medium.com/@TandemCapital/marketing-under-the-influence-social-media-superstars-as-a-marketing-channel-c8db4523588d

[131] Sinkwitz, J. (2016, September 19). Why should influencer marketing be a part of your strategy? Retrieved from https://blog.intellifluence.com/why-should-influencer-marketing-be-a-part-of-your-strategy-88122ece9dab

[132] Read, Ashley (2016, July 14). The complete guide to Instagram marketing. Retrieved from https://stories.buffer.com/the-complete-guide-to-instagram-marketing-a0ff0711bdc1?gi=d866af17eff5

Influencer Marketing[133], the company posits that worth of an Instagram post is a function of engagement rate [(likes+comments)/followers] with some sort of multiplier applied on the actual audience size to calculate engaged reach. That type of linear calculation is fair, but it falls apart at extremes when dealing with outliers

Photo 18.2 Credit: TBIT

like Kardashians and other celebs. If you're there, well … thank you for joining Intellifluence; let me get you a coffee. There isn't a true database of market rates for various activities and niches, but for your purposes, by engaging with others in your industry, you can get a rough feel for what an activity should cost.

If you can't (or don't) wish to engage with your peers, then you can base market rate on the average of your last five reviews for that niche opportunity and social platform. If you follow this metric, the TI would skew high in the very beginning since you'd need to build the experience and thus market rate would be close to zero. As you're experienced, you'll have enough of your own data (the best kind of data) to help guide market rate.

Let's calculate the TI for those three examples above:

New skin care influencer with zero similar posts

Value = $75

Fit = 1

Market Rate = $1

TI = (75*1)/1 = 75

Seasoned hair and beauty blogger with four similar posts

Value = $65

Fit = 0.75

Market Rate = $50

TI = (65*0.75)/50 = 0.975

Joe taking a look at the product, having never reviewed such a product before

Value = $50.10

Fit = 0.01

Market Rate = $1

TI = (50.01*0.01)/1 = 0.501

---

[133] Sinkwitz, J. (2017, January 5). The ultimate guide to using influencer marketing. Retrieved from https://blog.intellifluence.com/the-ultimate-guide-to-using-influencer-marketing-69021bae4b06

Cue hundreds of beauty and skin care brands hitting up my influencer profile now to be the first such brand I review.

From the calculations, we can see that it is painfully obvious that the new skin care influencer should jump at the opportunity. The decision is less clear for the seasoned hair and beauty blogger—if no other opportunities exist, then it is relevant enough to review, but not so much so that it is a "must" review. And, of course, there's little reason for me to do the review, even with me never having done such a review.

Now, keep in mind, if you're offered a significant sum on a low fit, it could still work, but the closer to 100 percent fit you get, the higher the TI becomes anyhow. What's beautiful about the simplicity of this reasoning is that as you become more authoritative, your fit as a percent will likely continue to remain high as the value offered to you increases. There may be errant opportunities pitched at a high enough value to still consider, but for the most part, you'll be benefiting from a positive feedback loop that keeps you focused and enriched.

RESPOND TO ALL PITCHES

I'll leave you with one more point. You are probably going to receive a significant volume of pitches over your career as an influencer, some not seemingly relevant and some perfect. Respond to all of them. Don't be afraid to negotiate. Don't be afraid to say no (but say something) and don't take offense if you receive a "low-ball" offer.

Photo 19.1 Credit: freestocks.org

CHAPTER 19

The Importance of Influencer Resistance

Becoming an authoritative influencer from scratch is not an easy process. Learn how to mentally handle the inevitable dips that occur, get inspired by how others who have dominated social influence before you came onto the scene, and understand that while it may take 10,000 hours of consistent effort before you're an expert, it'll only take 400 hours before you are not half bad.

While this chapter is a bit more of a standalone piece than some of the others, it would still be useful to read the following:

1. How to improve visibility[134]

2. How to determine what to focus on[135]

3. Optimizing your focus and visibility efforts[136]

4. Negotiating for fit over money initially to make more money long term[137]

The nature of this specific piece is designed to be something for you to read periodically when you are filled with self-doubt, when, despite your efforts, things don't seem to be going right.

TRIGGER WARNING: MOTIVATIONAL POST

Now, let's explore some realities.

Gigantic audiences on well-established platforms don't happen overnight. Building up the audience that you envision for yourself will take immense grit and perseverance to get through the dip that usually follows early growth. Let's be clear and realistic though; that dip is not the only dip you are going to encounter in this journey that you're on to becoming a full-time, ultra-high-paid influencer.

Photo 19.2 Credit: weknowmemes.com

There is no plateau; you have to keep moving. Think of the dips as a pause that follows early growth and precedes a more sustained and stronger growth. Andy Drish has a really good look into this phenomenon that he discovered after he made it through the dip[138] on his own business. He recognized that there wasn't a stopping point, a coasting on the beach plateau that he initially assumed there'd be after making it through the first dip. Instead, he found that one should expect a series of dips to occur over time, and that by meeting those adversities intelligently, one could overcome through refocus and reinvention.

---

[134] Sinkwitz, J. (2017, January 17). Becoming a top-tier influencer: Get visible. Retrieved from https://blog.intellifluence.com/becoming-a-top-tier-influencer-get-visible-c82867963e92e

[135] Sinkwitz, J. (2017, January 26). Becoming a top-tier influencer: Focus and authenticity. Retrieved from https://blog.intellifluence.com/becoming-a-top-tier-influencer-focus-and-authenticity-91b2ec154d0e

[136] Sinkwitz, J. (2017, February 1). Optimize your influence. Retrieved from https://blog.intellifluence.com/optimize-your-influence-6720367fce0e

[137] Sinkwitz, J. (2017, February 8). Influencers should negotiate, too. Retrieved from https://blog.intellifluence.com/influencers-should-negotiate-too-22490d1014f1

[138] Drish, A. (2016, January 7). The missing chapter of "the dip" every entrepreneur should know about. Retrieved from https://medium.com/hackerpreneur-magazine/the-missing-chapter-of-the-dip-every-entrepreneur-should-know-about-8942b4a3e934

Since I may have just played the role of Debbie Downer, I'll try to give you some motivation in the form of charts. Everyone starts somewhere and has to grow. Want proof? We're going to dive into some data sourced by the fantastic tool Social Blade (no relation to us, just a good tool).

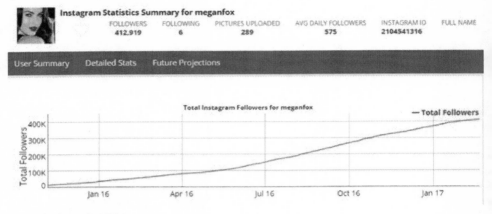

Graphic 19.1. Source: Social Blade

GET INSPIRED

You know Megan Fox? She's done a few movies. Well, did you know that her starting point on Instagram isn't a whole lot different than yours right now? Granted, her growth and popularity is a reflection of her offline activities, but this point is meant to show you just how much growth there can be ... zero to 400K in a little over a year. If she took Instagram as seriously as the last person in this exercise, she'd be 10 times that.

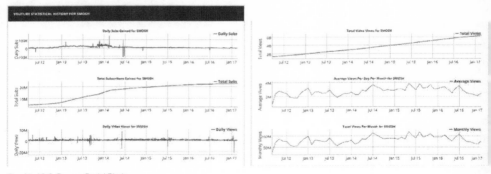

Graphic 19.2. Source: Social Blade

Next, we have the graphs for Smosh on YouTube. They provide a really interesting look at the various dips. Don't just look at the overall subscribers gained over time; look at average daily views and views per month. Yes, these ites are measured in millions, but they are spikey. Do you think his channel isn't constantly analyzing why it loses more than a million views in a given month? How much tweaking and reinvention has the channel undergone over the past couple of years to reach the success it currently enjoys?

And then there's Kylie Jenner.

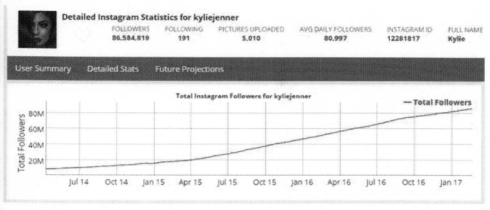

Graphic 19.3. Source: Social Blade

OK, OK. This one may seem unfair because it shows the Kylie had ~10M Instagram followers in 2014 and over 90M now. Which, let's say altogether, is i-n-s-a-n-e. This situation is actually more an example of what happens after making it through all the various dips—success can build upon itself at those upper levels, and the Kardashian-Jenner family absolutely treats social like a business ... a very lucrative business. She is unbelievably focused on constantly pushing to appeal to her audience and grow that audience, which is why her rates are several hundred thousand dollars minimum per campaign.

10,000 HOURS?

So how do you get from where you are to where they are? In an earlier piece, we referenced that approach. On the path to becoming an expert, one should expect to spend a significant amount of time—Malcom Gladwell refers to this scenario as the 10,000 hour to expertise approach. Obviously, if you're doing one hour a day of influencer reviews, that'd be a couple decades required to reach expertise.

Ain't nobody got time for that.

However, there's another way to approach, brought to us by Jon Collins. His theory is intriguing in that it takes 400 hours[139] to become "not half bad" at an activity. What Jon did here is combine the Pareto principle, otherwise known as the 80/20 rule, with Malcom's 10,000 hours guidance. This discussion is actually pretty important as an explanation because it shows that success is not binary: The more reviews you do, so long as you're willing to learn from your experiences in doing them, the more proficient you'll become. You'll see your competence and perceived value increase somewhat steadily until it increases exponentially when you reach expert status.

---

[139] Collins, J. (2015, October 15). Purposeful Pareto: 400 hours is all you need to become 'not half bad.' Retrieved from https://medium.com/@jonno/purposeful-pareto-400-hours-is-all-you-need-to-become-not-half-bad-896c6f4a0046

MY OWN JOURNEY

It wouldn't be a motivational post if I didn't share my own experiences. I have been involved in digital marketing — emphasis on search and now influencer marketing — since 1997. However, it wasn't until 2003 that I was recognized in any real capacity as being something of an expert. Once I was seen as an expert, it was crazy because my opportunities exploded[140], and as I've detailed on Steve Campbell's Ascent channel, it's resulted in an income I might not thought possible when I first started down this path. I'm not immune to my own dips — for instance, I still receive emails from people calling expertise into question, not understanding the parallels between search, social, paid advertising, and now influence. To overcome those questions, I need to keep creating useful information, be referenced by other experts as a fellow expert, and most importantly ... continue to put in the time required to maintain my expertise in the niche.

GET BACK TO YOUR JOURNEY

The break is over. It's time to get back to work. Keep pushing. If you are true to your focus and continue to provide a positive experience on the brands[141] you connect with, your audience and your opportunities will improve like mine did.

[140] Sinkwitz, J. (2016, August 12). Why I left a $250K/year CMO position to found a startup. Retrieved from https://theascent.biz/why-i-left-a-250k-yr-cmo-position-to-found-a-startup-fd9f617a8319

[141] Intellifluence (2016). Hello, brands. Retrieved from https://intellifluence.com/brands

Photo 20.1 Credit: kaboompics.com

CHAPTER 20

Top-Tier Influencers: Quality Over Quantity

Quality is a term too-often used without providing explanation. Understand how we define quality to mean depth of material using the humor niche as an example on YouTube with lip-reading dubs and crank calls, and then with children's book parodies on Twitter.

Now onto the next chapter of the influencer-centric section of the book, let the broken Sinkwitz record continue! We've covered at length the importance of keeping a focus[142], optimizing[143] for that focus, and remaining resilient[144] through the inevitable dips. Now, let us turn to the classic conundrum that faces all influencers: quality vs. quantity.

WHAT DOES QUALITY EVEN MEAN?

Quantity is a fairly well-established definition, meaning "how much" or "how many"—it is production volume. Quality is a fuzzier definition, though, since it varies significantly depending on who is assigning the label. For the purpose of this piece, consider quality to mean the addition of extra effort that results in a more finished product.

QUALITY VS. QUANTITY

Let's examine some comparable YouTube accounts to explore so we can see just how much of a difference there can be, exploring two niches that I personally subscribe to on YouTube, under the humor genre. Don't read too much into the obvious irreverence:

Lip-reading dubs. Note the difference on voice modulation, editing (or lack thereof), and video styling.

1. https://www.youtube.com/user/BadLipReading—More than 6 million subscribers, releasing over a couple videos per year, viewed as the top-tier dub channel. Each video is gold, and I watch them multiple times. Apparently, I'm not the only one.

2. https://www.youtube.com/user/Jabo0odyDubs— More than 1 million subscribers, these guys are a guilty pleasure of mine [NSFW unless you work in our office]. However, of the several videos per month, generally I really love one of them and end up sharing and watching it multiple times. Some of that repetition is a preference to dubbed infomercials over video game action, but also I think some is because the editing and dialogue on those product commercial dubs is superior vs. the improvisational styling of the video game dubs.

3. https://www.youtube.com/user/PimpedPistols—5.5 thousand subscribers [NSFW]. Some of it is funny, but much of the dubbing seems rushed. If it were to slow down and script a bit more to not repeat character dialogue, I'm pretty sure the subscriber account would jump as quality is so vital for YouTube. Compare this one to BadLipReading, which obviously has a lot more editing and production time baked into each video—the outcome is virality whereas this channel is still in an early discovery phase.

---

[142] Sinkwitz, J. (2017, January 26). Becoming a top-tier influencer: Focus and authenticity. Retrieved from https://blog.intellifluence.com/becoming-a-top-tier-influencer-focus-and-authenticity-91b2ec154d0e

[143] Sinkwitz, J. (2017, February 1). Optimize your influence. Retrieved from https://blog.intellifluence.com/optimize-your-influence-6720367fce0e

[144] Sinkwitz, J. (2017, February 21). The importance of influencer resilience. Retrieved from https://blog.intellifluence.com/the-importance-of-influencer-resilience-cd48ad5aca3b

Crank calls. *Voice + editing skills required like on dubs, but also requires animation skills as well.*

1. https://www.youtube.com/ownagepranks — 4.2 million subscribers. Now, what's a bit different here vs. the dubs channels is how much quality content they're able to put out, even at a higher than expected rate of production. As a disclaimer, they're in the Intellifluence network, and I love these guys. Hi Ed!

2. https://www.youtube.com/user/FridayNightCranks — 388,000 subscribers, with a couple of videos per month ... actually a bit less than Ownage. The call quality is good [and NSFW], but there's far less of the animation and other editing that makes for a polished piece.

As you can see in the selected examples, the more finished products that appear, that certain je nous sais quoi — the extra touches that separate a decent piece of content from a good piece of content. Do you have to choose between quality and quantity though? Ownage seems capable of doing more, better, but if they had to choose, I would imagine the choice for them would be to focus on fewer good cranks and pranks than a higher volume of average quality videos.

In some channels like Twitter, the quality wouldn't seem as important at first glance, since 140 characters is not a high bar, content-wise. I'll caution comedic Twitter influencers[145] though. If you were to put out one good joke and 100 bad jokes, the probability of losing subscribers is higher than if you just put out two good jokes and nothing else. Don't believe me?

TWITTER QUALITY VS. QUANTITY

Keeping with the comedic themes of dubs and cranks, the two-dimensional and static version would be artistic parodies, specifically, in this case, children's book cover parodies[146].

1. https://twitter.com/paprbckparadise — 137,000 followers, and frankly it should be more because they are almost all incredible. As a relatively newer account with a solid volume of continual parody book covers, I expect 2017 to be a breakout year. Some of these parodies are poster worthy: 10/10 — would subscribe again.

2. https://twitter.com/maryanne_spier — 562 followers and possibly not the best comparison since the parodies are far and few between, mostly just riffing on storylines without the supporting imagery. The jokes themselves aren't all bad, so I can't help but wonder what the subscriber count would be with that supportive imagery to solicit sharing. I chose to include this account as a comparison not to pick on it, but to reiterative the importance of focus. Paperback Paradise is extremely

---

[145] Intellifluence (2016). Hello, influencers. Retrieved from https://intellifluence.com/influencers/

[146] Know Your Meme (2014). Children's book cover parodies. Retrieved from http://knowyourmeme.com/memes/childrens-book-cover-parodies

focused on the parodies whereas Maryanne only occasionally drops in the joke storylines.

WHAT ABOUT BLOGS?

The quality vs. quantity conundrum is more difficult when looking at blogs. It's tricky because traffic, links, and engagement signals to blog posts change with consumer tastes. Where I enjoy deep content with supporting data on case studies, such as the material that John-Henry Scherck puts out for DocSend[147], occasionally an article on what Larry Page had for lunch and its implications on the

Graphic 20.1. Source: Flickeringmyth.com

next big search update ends up being initially more popular despite its empty value.

The great equalizer in this case is time. Quality comes into play because the DocSend piece will be significantly more evergreen, thus earning more links and shares for a considerable period of time. This situation would help it to overtake whatever initial signal spikes might occur compared with the other industry filler piece posted on a more widely read publication. The example isn't perfect, but as a takeaway, focusing on quality can win in the end over vacuous posts which are created at spam-canon scale and forgotten two weeks later.

SO QUALITY OR QUANTITY?

The more involved the medium (see above for YouTube on the various skills required),

the more necessary it is to be hyper-focused on quality versus how many pieces can be produced. The same is actually true even for those on Twitter, where additional effort pays off over time, though arguably less important since fewer skills are required to make a good or even great piece of content.

All this said, a top-tier influencer cares more about the value provided to his or her audience, which is why quality is so important. The ego metrics of like, follow, share, replies, etc. are great for determining engagement and rabidity of fans when brands are seeking out such influences, but these areas are just a byproduct of producing quality work than the product itself. If you focus on making something great for your audience, you'll inadvertently hit all the metrics you need to be sought out by the brands you hope to one day work with.

---

[147] Scherck, J. (2016, October 18). 150+ of the best case study examples for B2B product marketers. Retrieved from https://www.docsend.com/best-b2b-case-study-examples/

Photo 21.1 Credit: rawpixel.com

CHAPTER 21

Hey Influencers, Listen to Your Audience!

Feedback is critical for any influencer looking to improve. Learn first how to solicit internal feedback, how to listen to unsolicited feedback, and how to engage with your audience for feedback purposes.

While the influencer resilience[148] chapter was designed to build you up when you're frustrated, this chapter is designed to keep you grounded. I like to think of this chapter as the "get your sh*t together" companion piece to that chapter. If you're losing your audience, don't cast blame; rather, be retrospective about it.

GET SOME INTERNAL FEEDBACK

There are multiple ways to gauge audience feedback. If you have thin skin, the first way is to self-diagnose for feedback. It isn't optimal as a complete solution, but can be useful as a starting point toward continual improvement. Let's look at some questions you can ask yourself. Remember, this item all needs to tie back to what you are optimizing[149] for as you seek to maximize your post quality[150].

Are your posts too frequent?

Buffer has an interesting post on post frequency[151], wherein they attempt to break down posting by how many times a day you should post on various social channels and by time of day. As a nerd, my favorite part is the reference of Dan Wilkerson because Dan's post from several years back still holds true. You can read the full piece here[152], but the main takeaway is that the optimum frequency can't really be guessed—you need to test. Does this point take you back to high school chemistry class: setting up a hypothesis to test, measuring observations, and coming to a conclusion? By endeavoring to test and measuring the results on what happens if you post more, or less, or at different times a day, you can better determine if you're shooting yourself in the foot or not. If engagement changes (both comment frequency and tone); follower counts change; likes, shares, retweets, etc. change, then you have something actionable to work with.

Are your posts fragmented by industry, showing a lack of focus or authenticity[153]?

Obviously, we've covered this point multiple times now, but by bringing it up again, hopefully you understand how serious we are about this. If your sample of 10 posts is one sunglasses product review, two posts about your children, three obviously paid blog posts referencing online casinos and payday loans, and five on skin care products but you want to review sunglasses for a living, something has to change. I can joke about that point a little, because there was a time where I was the one buying those spammy blog posts from you.

[148] Sinkwitz, J. (2017, February 21). The importance of influencer resilience. Retrieved from https://blog.intellifluence.com/the-importance-of-influencer-resilience-cd48ad5aca3b

[149] Sinkwitz, J. (2017, February 1). Optimize your influence. Retrieved from https://blog.intellifluence.com/optimize-your-influence-6720367fce0e

[150] Sinkwitz, J. (2017, February 27). Top-tier influencers: Quality over quantity. Retrieved from https://blog.intellifluence.com/top-tier-influencers-quality-over-quantity-e77662e74c79

[151] Lee, K. (2016, August 29). How often to post to Facebook, Twitter, LinkedIn and more. Retrieved from https://stories.buffer.com/how-often-to-post-to-facebook-twitter-linkedin-and-more-bb2758459162

[152] Wilkerson, D. (2013, August 19). How often should I post on Facebook or Twitter? Retrieved from http://www.lunametrics.com/blog/2013/08/19/frequency-post-facebook-twitter/

[153] Sinkwitz, J. (2017, January 26). Becoming a top-tier influencer: Focus and authenticity. Retrieved from https://blog.intellifluence.com/becoming-a-top-tier-influencer-focus-and-authenticity-91b2ec154d0e

Does your 10-post sample pass the sniff test? You want someone who doesn't know you to be able to quickly glance at the sample set, and by word association, be able to say what your social channel or persona is about. In this case, it likely wouldn't be "sunglasses influencer."

Are your posts counter to the ideals of your audience (such as political, geocentric, etc)?

1. Politics is a pretty obvious consideration considering how polarized we are in the United States right now. If you're that sunglasses influencer, and every other post is about Donald Trump, you are probably turning off 60 percent of your audience. Likewise, if you hold the oppositional political view and post about it frequently, you may be losing 40 percent of your audience ... permanently. I won't say that you shouldn't be involved politically or have views. Just be aware that simply by stating your views where sides exist and lines are drawn that you will immediately alienate a portion of the audience, for better or worse.

2. Geography is another important factor. Like politics, if you are always posting your sunglasses reviews in a Yankees hat, you probably won't sell too much to your audience in Boston. Understanding where your audience lives and who they are is vital. We preached that brands get a better understanding of who they are trying to influence; the lessons in that article[154] are applicable to you as well. The article covers a wide variety of cultural and psychological factors. If you really want to understand your audience, dig deep on it.

HOW TO LISTEN AND HANDLE EXTERNAL FEEDBACK

Maybe your skin is a bit thicker, or maybe you're committed to success. If so, then it is time to learn how to listen to feedback. It can come from multiple angles: direct emails, comments on your threads, subtweeted by haters, word of mouth, broadcasted on "Saturday Night Live," etc. However it comes in, you need to learn how to process. Who better to listen to that than Gary Vaynerchuk in his thesis on how to handle feedback.[155]

OK, now that you get how to strip the emotionality from the feedback, it's still time to actually listen. Nicole Williams has a short and sweet methodology:[156]

1. Listen, without explaining—just shut up and listen.

2. Decide whether or not you agree with the criticism—is the person hating on you or is he or she providing a possible critique?

[154] Sinkwitz, J. (2016, October 5). Who exactly are you trying to influence? Retrieved from https://blog.intellifluence.com/who-are-you-trying-to-influence-ba8ddaf5a575

[155] Vaynerchuk, G. (2016, May 17). My thesis on how to handle feedback. Retrieved from https://medium.com/@garyvee/my-thesis-on-how-to-handle-feedback-d385406fcaf

[156] Williams, N. (2016, October 19). How to welcome feedback (advice from a fellow perfectionist). Retrieved from https://medium.com/@envycollect/how-to-welcome-feedback-advice-from-a-fellow-perfectionist-bc81b58c9ca2

3. If the criticism is valid, is it something you can actually address or is it out of your control? If it is out of your control, then beyond thanking them for the feedback, there isn't much use losing sleep.

4. If the criticism got past all those filters, what is your resolution to correcting it?

The process is great because it allows you to ignore the negative sentiment as Gary suggests and just approach the feedback logically. I won't lie; it isn't easy. We have almost 30,000 influencers[157] as I edit this chapter and close to 2,500 brands[158] using our system to date, so as you can imagine, we get a large amount of feedback — some is easy to take and some isn't, especially if I made the decision to do something specific that turns out to be universally hated. I will say that, over time, as you encounter more and more feedback, so long as you can emotionally detach yourself from the feedback, it becomes easier to process and becomes one of the most valued channels you have when it comes to improvement.

HOW TO INTERACT WITH YOUR AUDIENCE FOR FEEDBACK PURPOSES

Now that understand how to handle the feedback as it comes in, let's go get some. There are a few takeaways I'd like you to focus on.

1. Be responsive. There's a saying in baseball: speed kills. It's not the best analogy here; I just like it and was light on my sports analogy quota, having only referenced the Yankees and Red Sox rivalry. Seriously, though, the quicker you are to respond to comments on your channels and emails, the better. Quick answers spur more conversation and conversation spurs more eyeballs. In other words, by being quick to get back to your fans and casual engagers, you're building your audience.

2. Direct questions to the audience. Ask for their opinions; call them out. If you have regular commenters, name drop them, give them exposure, and watch how far they're willing to spread your message for you. By directly engaging them, you are changing the overall makeup of your channels, which leads to the next point.

3. The goal is to make them feel like your channel is as much their home as it is yours, and you'll be seen less as a broadcaster and more of a community leader.

Photo 21.2 Credit: tigerstrypes.com

[157] Intellifluence (2016). Welcome, influencers. Retrieved from https://intellifluence.com/influencers
[158] Intellifluence (2016). Hello, brands. Retrieved from https://intellifluence.com/brands

This point will lead to much clearer and honest feedback and make the experience better for everyone. Plus, they'll be more likely to perform desired actions on your reviews, which will lead to higher brand satisfaction, more money, planetary harmony, and universal acclaim. *Cough* Too obscure of a joke? I should have stopped at more money.

Now go and be excellent to your audience.

Photo 22.1 Credit: DepositPhotos.com by dashek

CHAPTER 22

Be in the Know, Be First, or Be Best

Breaking news isn't always the best strategy for influencers. Learn, using a lesson from content marketing, the differences and advantages or disadvantages to being the fastest, the most accurate, or simply the best influencer for a niche.

As we discussed previously, one way to build a bigger audience is by engaging with and listening to that audience[159]. One way to get more engagement is to be top of mind, and there are a few ways to do that. If you can be more in the know than your fellow industry influencers[160], you can be faster to break industry news and the first to review products within your chosen niche, or you can simply be the best.

In journalism, yes even in this weird post-facts world we're temporarily living in, there are typically two winners: the first to report and the most accurate reporting. Think about how this point works in the world of journalism, as it applies to social media. The news outlet that breaks a story is generally cited by those piling on later with their commentary, which leads to a downhill rolling snowball of publicity and coverage for the reporter and outlet. The tricky aspect, which we've all become more and more sensitive to, is whether in the rush to be first some of the details discussed end up being not entirely accurate, resulting in future retractions. Conversely, the most accurate reporting is rarely the fastest, but well after the news cycle, it becomes the secondary piece referenced by those researching a story.

It is at this point that one can add an addendum to first or accurate, and that addendum is to be the best. Josh Stearns has an interesting selection process on his best lists of journalism[161] by year, and if you read through any of them, you'll find a theme: These best pieces are exceptionally thorough and detail a level of knowledge on the subject matter that you very rarely find on the "breaking" pieces, and they are still a rarity on those that tend to win for accuracy.

SEGUE TO CONTENT MARKETING

Those of you that know me know that I have a fairly long history throughout digital marketing that starts in hypercompetitive search and layered on content marketing as we moved up the value chain. I'm segueing to content marketing because there's an interesting parallel to journalism, and then from there, to influencer marketing (which is why you're here of course).

In content marketing, there's the concept of the trifecta, which is outlined nicely by Tyler Hakes of Optimist[162]. Distilled down to its basics, the trifecta is essentially looking at three types of content necessary for a winning strategy: evergreen content, social and viral content, and link-earning content.

Social/viral content. This area is fairly self-explanatory, the ephemeral content that is more emotionally-centric than informational usually. The point of this type of content is usually

[159] Sinkwitz, I. (2017, March 8). Hey influencers, listen to your audience! Retrieved from https://blog.intellifluence.com/hey-influencers-listen-to-your-audience-6eb59ebfee6c

[160] Intellifluence (2016). Welcome, influencers. Retrieved from https://intellifluence.com/influencers

[161] Stearns, J. (2017, January 4). A roadmap to the best journalism of 2016. Retrieved from https://medium.com/@jcstearns/a-roadmap-to-the-best-journalism-of-2016-7ae929207b97

[162] Hakes, T. (n.d.). How we scaled a startup from 0 organic traffic to 100,000 visitors per month (in about one year). Retrieved from http://yesoptimist.com/content-marketing-seo-case-study-the-trifecta-strategy/

to maximize spread, the broadest type of net casting as far as content is concerned. The parallel to journalism here is that of being first. The first story usually goes the furthest due to its breaking nature and neither are judged particularly harshly on accuracy.

Evergreen content. Evergreen content answers a question, preferably when the answer doesn't frequently change. While evergreen content is sometimes viewed as boring, it serves its purpose in satisfying search users. The journalistic analogy here is that of being the most factually accurate, used as a reference.

Link-earning content. This area is where the magic happens. Link-earning content is typically really useful, factual, and somewhat sharable, hence its ability to earn links. As you might have guessed, the parallel to journalism is the remaining example, the best journalistic piece.

Photo 22.2 Credit: Kaboompics.com

Why would I segue to content marketing like that? Well, many of you are bloggers, and in between wanting to help you grow your social audiences, I'd love to see your blogs flourish as well. Additionally, the analogy of first, most accurate, and best carries into influencer success as well. Now that you have a good feel for how the three work, we can approach this point as a how-to experiment.

BECOMING THE FASTEST AND BREAKING INFLUENCER

By staying on top of industry news and reading up on the various posts and books that come out of your niche, you increase the probability that you are not only one of the best informed influencer, but you also may be the one to break a story on a hot new product with the first review.

How can you stay on top of the news?

1. Google alerts. These alerts are pretty simple to set up. You can set up an alert for literally any keyword combination: a person's name, a brand name, an adjective, etc.

2. Brand24 is partner to us and has its own Google Alerts alternative[163] that allows you to track with much greater detail.

3. RSS feeds. If you're in most modern blogs and forums for your niche, you can look for the RSS button and add that content to your Chrome or FireFox browser with ease. I find this tool to be quicker than using Google Alerts, since there can sometimes be significant delays and also because private forums generally aren't available to Google's index.

---

[163] Brand24 (2017, February 23). Google Alerts alternative. Retrieved from https://medium.com/@brand24/google-alerts-alternative-7505be30fa4c

4. Cision NA. Cision has a lot of uses in the PR world, but for today's purpose, you can use it in a similar to Google Alerts but with more horsepower, as Cision sees press releases as they come through the system and can parse them for the keywords that interest you most.

5. Twitter and Instagram hashtag stalking. If you're stalking #keto, you probably saw my fabulous video. No? Well, it was fun to do. Now, you could hashtag stalk via the alerts above, or you could do another fun thing by consuming feeds[164] in Slack.

BECOMING THE MOST ACCURATE INFLUENCER

This one is hard, but it is all about depth and exploration. In order to become the most accurate influencer, you need to know how to perform research[165] and ask the right questions. As you go down the arduous path of consistently researching your subjects, beware of this pitfall[166] shared by First Draft. If your goal is to be seen as the most accurate influencer, you must ensure that you never lose the trust of your audience because it will be exceptionally difficult to get it back.

BECOMING THE BEST INFLUENCER

This item goes back to the quality > quantity[167] chapter. In some ways, I think it is also a function of combining some of the above elements. The best influencers in a niche are not only going to be accurate (but I think they absolutely should be since the FTC sees this as a form of advertising), but they also need to be creating something that is sharable (see viral content above) and it needs to be timely (that is, breaking news if possible). In other words, the best influencers by niche are unicorns. They are providing the breaking news product reviews, accurately, and in a fun way that encourages the review to spread. That's certainly something to strive for. Do this and the competition doesn't stand a chance.

---

[164] Slack (2015, April 6). Integrations 101: Adding Twitter to Slack. Retrieved from https://slackhq.com/integrations-101-adding-twitter-to-slack-d7a46b5425d0?gi=9f8926ab0efe

[165] ThePensters (2015, December 15). An in-depth manual on how to write a research paper. Retrieved from https://medium.com/@ThePensters/an-in-depth-manual-on-how-to-write-a-research-paper-5b7a59a2f8f3

[166] Stearns, J. (2016, May 27). How journalists build and break trust with their audience online. Retrieved from https://medium.com/1st-draft/how-journalists-build-and-break-trust-with-their-audience-online-9f6938b28479

[167] Sinkwitz, J. (2017, February 27). Top-tier influencers: Quality over quantity. Retrieved from https://blog.intellifluence.com/top-tier-influencers-quality-over-quantity-e77662e74c79

Photo 23.1. Credit: Kaboompics.com

CHAPTER 23

Community & Collaboration

Using travel industry influencers as an example, explore how to involve your broader niche community into your overall practice, trading leads in order to remain focused, collaborating to improve quality, and simply looking out for each other.

Hearkening back to our kickoff piece on gaining visibility[168] and optimizing for that visibility[169], this chapter is about growth; it also builds upon the necessity of listening to one's audience[170] because many of those skills are required. It is important to not see yourself as a lonely product review stuck on a deserted island. You are a part of a community, and you can lean on that community to improve and expand.

WHAT IS THIS COMMUNITY YOU SPEAK OF?

Let's pretend you're a travel writer. Been anywhere awesome lately? Care to share your itinerary with the world?

The travel world is big — really, really big. There are many very large companies that are extremely interested in hiring travel influencers[171] to describe in detail a variety of travel-related items. While you may travel extensively, is it possible that you're an expert on Munich museum attractions, where to get the best street tacos in Guadalajara, which are the hidden gem hotels in Jabalpur, and how to maximize airline points using mall gift cards? If you actually can do all that, I tip my invisible hat, but the point is to express how deep the industry is. The deeper an industry is, the more likely there is specialization, and therefore the more important it is that as you seek to become an expert[172] in your specific niche, that you cultivate relationships with other tangential experts. This is the community that you need to become a part of, whether your motivations are selfish or altruistic.

ISN'T COMMUNITY ANOTHER WORD FOR COMPETITOR?

In a way, yes. There's a lot of different words for this term. Steve Blank of Startup Grind would refer to such network relationships as frenemies[173], though I think in this case that might not be the best analogy because that relationship probably more closely mirrors being an embedded influencer on ongoing brand campaigns where one party is clearly working for another and both want to ensure that maximum value extraction takes place from their own personal perspectives. Instead, I would view your niche industry community to be more the coopetition in this approach, as described by Dan Brown in his post on creative couples[174]. I'm not suggesting you get romantically involved, but if a wedding occurs because of Intellifluence, I sure want to know about it so I can retweet your registry.

---

[168] Sinkwitz, J. (2017, January 17). Becoming a top-tier influencer: Get visible. Retrieved from https://blog.intellifluence.com/becoming-a-top-tier-influencer-get-visible-c8286796392e

[169] Sinkwitz, J. (2017, February 1) Optimize your influence. Retrieved from https://blog.intellifluence.com/optimize-your-influence-6720367fce0e

[170] Sinkwitz, J. (2017, March 8). Hey influencers, listen to your audience! Retrieved from https://blog.intellifluence.com/hey-influencers-listen-to-your-audience-6eb59ebfee6c

[171] Intellifluence (2016). Welcome, influencers. Retrieved from https://intellifluence.com/influencers

[172] Sinkwitz, J. (2017, February 21). The importance of influencer resilience. Retrieved from https://blog.intellifluence.com/the-importance-of-influencer-resilience-cd48ad5aca3b

[173] Blank, S. (2017, February 3). VC's are not your friends, they're frenemies. Retrieved from https://medium.com/startup-grind/vcs-are-not-your-friends-they-re-frenemies-e3dacb9be631

[174] Brown, D. (2015, March 16). Coopetition. Retrieved from https://medium.com/@brownorama/if-my-occasional-tweets-and-instagram-posts-about-it-haven-t-convinced-you-r-m-loving-joshua-wolf-ef138393968e

Instead, it is about the "infinite game," where the point is to keep moving the game forward for everyone in a way that ensures everyone succeeds at least enough to keep playing. You want to help your peers to keep playing the review game.

Why should you help potential competitors grow? I ran across something from Evan Carmichael that sums it up. I'm not a big Tony Robbins guy, but this point is accurate[175]. The theory goes that you are the average of your five closest peers. The better your peer group is doing, the better you're doing.

HOW CAN YOU HELP YOUR COMMUNITY?

If you're convinced now that it is generally in your best interest to help the sum total of your niche industry, the next question falls to how to get that done. There are quite a few ways:

1. Lead flow. Remember earlier when we talked about the difficulty of being an expert on everything travel-related? Let's say you are really great at finding those street tacos, but don't know much about India. Now, if you're contacted by a travel brand that really needs to have itineraries built out for awesome India trips, the simple way you can assist the community is getting the right people connected

Photo 23.2. Credit: Tim Gouw

to ensure the brand is taken care of and that your peer expert with the India knowledge gets some additional work. This type of community benefit is also very obvious because the law of reciprocity comes into play; by helping someone, that person is going to be more likely to help you in the future if a brand comes to this individual needing help with street taco content. Additionally, the brand you helped will remember you as the helpful travel influencer and think "maybe she knows everyone" and begins coming to you at the outset of all requests.

2. Community protection. I hate that this element is even a thing that I need to write about. Recently, someone signed up as a brand and chose to indiscriminately message more than 600 influencers with a pitch[176] that caused some influencers to feel a sense of disgust and leave the network. Only through the quick action of John Clark of Yofreesamples.com were we made aware of the issue and were able to take action to boot the brand from the network within the hour of notification. When these things occur, we can get negative reviews in response, but our promise

[175] Carmichael, E. (2015, September 24). "People's lives are a direct reflection of the expectations of their peer groups." Retrieved from https://medium.com/@EvanCarmichael/people-s-lives-are-a-direct-reflection-of-the-expectations-of-their-peer-group-e8de8327988a
[176] Sinkwitz, J. (2016, October 31). How to pitch influencers. Retrieved from https://blog.intellifluence.com/how-to-pitch-influencers-5b2dd319a0c6

is to protect the integrity of the network and ensure the community is not abused. It is worth the negative reviews to be able to point to us actually caring about the people we work with. It's a long side note, but by reporting issues of abuse, you are making the network more valuable to everyone that uses it. This point extends to other networks and community forums where you interact—if someone or something is taking advantage of the community or one of its members, speak up so appropriate action can be taken.

3. *Collaboration*. This area is one of those mutual benefit scenarios, both altruistic and selfish. By suggesting the inclusion of other influencers on a project, you are potentially turning a simple campaign into a richer, more immersive campaign. Multiple influencers means more than just the sum of the audience sizes, because through psychology of touchpoints, seeing a message multiple times creates a greater neuro imprint to a potential consumer. Also, chained campaigns are sexy to brands right now, as they more closely resemble traditional Madison Avenue ad campaigns. This point also fits into lead flow. It isn't just a matter of agreeing to work with someone else, but actively suggest it as a means to make the campaign more of a win.

WHERE ARE THESE MYTHICAL COMMUNITIES?

I'm not a travel influencer, but with some quick searching, I found a great number of places that travelers hang out—if you're in the space, maybe consider them:

- http://www.travbuddy.com/forums
- http://www.travellerspoint.com/forum.cfm
- https://www.reddit.com/r/travel/
- http://www.wanderlust.co.uk/mywanderlust/

Photo 24.1. Credit: DepositPhotos.com by DmitryPoch

CHAPTER 24

Influencer Outreach, for Influencers

Outreach is not an activity that should be left only to brands and their agencies. Learn how to apply a series of tactics designed to help you stand out from your influencer peers, why you need to be ever-present, and when you might want to consider getting trained.

In our previous chapter on interacting with your niche community and collaboration[177], one of the reasons to work with your frenemies and the coopetition was to increase visibility[178]. Being seen is such a large component of becoming a top-tier influencer[179] that I wanted to delve into how one can go about pushing that visibility further, since so many brands in our network[180] and others will claim that audience visibility is the top selection factor when evaluating influencers.

FIRST, GET NOTICED

What are the various ways to get noticed? If you really break it down, like Brendan McCaughey does here[181], then the ways to stick out are to:

1. *Work harder in comparison to one's peers.* This one makes sense right? All things being equal, the person who is simply trying harder and doing more is going to be at an advantage of being seen than one's peer. It is a sheer numbers game, a matter of probability. Being in a position to be noticed more frequently will result, statistically, in being noticed more.

2. *Be different in some way.* I liken this one a bit to what we suggest on the importance of focus and authenticity. Using one's own voice and digging deep on a specific topic sets one apart from the homogeneity that is generalized product reviews.

3. *Make eye contact.* Or maybe in the case of digital influence, we can associate the concept to the ability to send direct messages, pick up the phone, or, more literally, look into the camera on Skype. Our closest analogies really exist to try to provide as close a physical connection as possible. They aren't quite the same as looking a person in the eye when talking, so this is close as we can get to take the additional step of contact.

4. *Keep learning.* This advice fits neatly with what we've previously discussed on resilience on the 10,000 hours theory and Pareto principle, moving from not-half-bad to expert.

Once you are capable of being noticed, you need to apply pressure and push to gain that attention.

HOW CAN I GET NOTICED?

[177] Sinkwitz, J. (2017, March 22). Community & collaboration. Retrieved from https://blog.intellifluence.com/community-collaboration-42ae57a1f2a0

[178] Sinkwitz, J. (2017, January 17). Becoming a top-tier influencer: Get visible. Retrieved from https://blog.intellifluence.com/becoming-a-top-tier-influencer-get-visible-c8286796392e

[179] Intellifluence (2016). Welcome, influencers. Retrieved from https://intellifluence.com/influencers

[180] Intellifluence (2016). Hello, brands. Retrieved from https://intellifluence.com/brands

[181] McCaughey, B. (2017, March 9). A beginners guide to getting noticed. Retrieved from https://medium.com/@multitude27/a-beginners-guide-to-getting-noticed-76f5f8c4fc91

Photo 24.2. Credit: William Iven

Sometimes, the best way to grow an audience is to get noticed off the platform. What do I mean by off-platform attention that drives on-platform audience growth? Paul Kemp shares some of the successes he had a few years ago as an example[182]. Note the traffic impact he had by leveraging where he was already seeing a little attention and turning it into a lot of attention.

That traffic and extra attention cycled back around to grow his platform audiences to a significant degree.

SERIOUSLY, HOW CAN I GET NOTICED?

OK. OK. Let's start by looking at how to guest post anywhere[183], which comes to us from our friend John Rampton. I recommend that you read his post in detail, but there are a few very straightforward takeaways. As an order of operations:

1. Make sure you already have a blog with high-quality content. *cough* That means quality over quantity.

2. Find places you can guest blog on. John breaks out a couple different ways to go about this process using a few tools like Sitecomber and some basic Google queries. Keep in mind that not all of these sites are going to be relevant. In fact, I would say that most probably aren't; however, some of the larger generalized publications might still be a fit.

3. Dig further on specific personality and niche queries with "guest post" keyword modifiers to see where your industry authoritative influencers are hanging out. Remember, co-citation is a big deal. If you can appear alongside the experts, then before you know it, you will start to be perceived as an expert.

4. Use a tool like Buzzstream and LinkedIn to try and identify who the editors and guest blog account holders are.

5. Research like an influencer on a mission. Look into comments, aged blog posts that aren't correct, etc. You need ideas on what you want to provide.

6. Pitch. One of the most popular posts on our blog is how to pitch, and it doesn't

[182] Kemp, P. (2015, October 31). A crazy week getting noticed by the tech press. Retrieved from https://medium.com/@TheAppGuy/a-crazy-week-of-getting-noticed-by-the-tech-press-b113d6bb50df

[183] Rampton, J. (2015, September 24) How to guest blog anywhere. Retrieved from https://www.johnrampton.com/how-to-guest-post-anywhere/

really even deal with content pitches, but all the advice is still applicable on developing a concise value-providing pitch.

7. A variant on the above exercise is getting interviews via sheer hustle explained by Jeff Bullas on his tips to becoming an industry influencer[184]. The variant essentially is basically "industry" and "interview" search queries, and then following through on the above steps since you'll still need to provide a compelling pitch on why you should be interviewed. The more work that you can do for the editor or author, the more likely it is that you'll get an accepted pitch.

BE EVERYWHERE

Pushing hard to get guest posting opportunities and interviews is a solid strategy. I've used it to a degree several times for various businesses. So long as you put in the required work, you'll see results. While this strategy is all occurring, though, you need to stay as active as possible on as many networks as possible. As Roberto Blake would suggest, you need to appear everywhere[185]. In his methodology, it can be broken down in digestible chunks of time to prevent rabbit holing on topics unnecessarily. Being everywhere once casts the perception of always being in the thick of the discussion, which results in publications pitching you to do interviews and guest posts. There's no greater compliment you can receive than "how many people are you, really?"

GET TRAINED

It is easier for me to dole out advice than it is to make it work, because there are lots of moving pieces in establishing yourself as I so casually suggest. Thus, another avenue is to consider getting professionally trained by a PR expert[186] like Mary Simms. The lines between influencers and public relations professionals are getting blurred, so by better understanding the ins and outs of public relations and key publications as it pertains to your niche, you can inject yourself into the conversation in a way that greatly benefits you, building up both your off-platform and on-platform reach, translating into the significant audience growth that you and brands want to see.

[184] Bullas, J. (n.d.) 7 tips to become an influencer in your industry. Retrieved from http://www.jeffbullas.com/7-tips-become-influencer-industry/

[185] Blake. R. (2017, January 16). Can you really be everywhere at once in #socialmedia? Retrieved from https://medium.com/@robertoblake/can-you-really-be-everywhere-at-once-in-socialmedia-9c0500941117

[186] Simms, M. (n.d.) Empowering authors. Retrieved from http://prinfluencers.com/10-weeks-to-media-mentions/

Photo 25.1. Credit: freestockpro.com

CHAPTER 25

Want Hyper Growth? Adopt Early

Some amount of audience growth potential boils down to being in the right place at the right time. By using a helpful heuristic, learn how to determine if it is too early when adopting new social networks as part of your routine or if a network has entered the Goldilocks zone for your niche.

We've gone over several methods to help you grow your audience, from basic visibility tips[187] and optimization[188] to working with the coopetition[189] and doing outreach[190]. One item that is often neglected, though, is a very simple tactic: early adoption of new platforms.

WHY ADOPT EARLY?

Being an early player on a new network gives you a visibility advantage relative to mature networks, simply on a numbers basis. Being one of 100,000 is very different than being one of 100 million. If the smaller network you identify and put actual effort into should manage to go from 100,000 to 1 million or 10 million, you will almost certainly see your personal audience increase accordingly, and you can translate back to your other network profiles as friends and followers that discover you on the new platform and will be more willing to also follow you on the existing, mature platforms.

HOW ABOUT AN EXAMPLE?

As an example of this point, look at the story of Vine. Vine is ideal for a couple of reasons:

1. It offered an explosion of growth where new talent was discovered due to the novel concept of short-format videos that attracted new social media users.

2. Post-acquisition, it was completely neglected and was effectively shelved after languishing, no matter how Twitter management chooses to spin it, which was just a colossal mistake. Steve Bowbrick knows[191] what I'm talking about.

3. The smart influencers[192] who built large audiences on Vine translated that success over onto more mature platforms like YouTube, Facebook, Instagram, and into other new networks like Snapchat. Someone without a meaningful following pre-Vine who managed to build a solid audience which was migrated over time onto YouTube and Facebook is absolutely cleaning up now with Facebook Live[193] videos as recommended by Rebekah Radice, and if such an influencer doubled down on the time investment to push original content on Snapchat, which syndicates back into YouTube, is probably seeing a continuing growth trend. The time investment probably isn't even that different than before since the efforts put into Vine could be

[187] Sinkwitz, J. (2017, January 17). Becoming a top-tier influencer: Get visible. Retrieved from https://blog.intellifluence.com/becoming-a-top-tier-influencer-get-visible-c8286796392e

[188] Sinkwitz, J. (2017, February 1). Optimize your influence. Retrieved from https://blog.intellifluence.com/optimize-your-influence-6720367fce0e

[189] Sinkwitz, J. (2017, March 22). Community & collaboration. Retrieved from https://blog.intellifluence.com/community-collaboration-42ae57a1f2a0

[190] Sinkwitz, J. (2017, March 28). Influencer outreach, for influencers. Retrieved from https://blog.intellifluence.com/influencer-outreach-for-influencers-266fd4bfcafa

[191] Bowbrick, S. (2016, November 4). How is this only six seconds? Retrieved from https://medium.com/@bowbrick/how-is-this-only-six-seconds-a37cbcafab2a

[192] Intellifluence (2016). Welcome, influencers. Retrieved from https://intellifluence.com/influencers

[193] Radice, R. (2016, November 11). 4 ways to leverage Facebook Live. Retrieved from https://medium.com/@RebekahRadice/4-ways-to-leverage-facebook-live-494b38223159

dropped for a different network.

HOW EARLY IS TOO EARLY?

I'm going to skip the discussion on how to find new networks, because it is almost a mistake to actively try to find them. Listen to your audience[194] on where they spend their time and keep an ear open in your niche communities — that's sufficient.

Photo 25.2. Credit: startupstockphotos.com

Instead, we should discuss when early is too early. It is a classic question, whether it pertains to Jason M. Lemkin's advice on when to hire key executives[195], whether to invest in an industry, or when to focus time and investment in a new social network. As Michael Dempsey would argue, all things being equal, it is better to be too early than too late[196]. To help find that magical balance, let's create a rough heuristic. The idea behind this heuristic is to determine when you should probably jump into a network head first and consider it a part of your everyday influence routine. This item is just my heuristic which I find helpful in determining whether I'm going to be wasting my time or if I might be finding that shining needle in the proverbially noisy haystack.

1. IF the new network has at least 10 active accounts that you're connected to already on other accounts, AND you believe those accounts are actually worth following, go to step 2.

2. IF the new network is doing something novel (that is, not just a pure copycat of an existing network), go to step 3.

3. IF the new network would result in relevant followers for you to apply influence on, due to it being accepting both for your niche as well as having an audience that would seek out your niche, set up an account.

4. IF new account does not translate into growth of real, non-bot accounts (on the new network) within two weeks, hold on to those activities and try again two months later. Keep repeating for six months.

[194] Sinkwitz, J. (2017, March 8). Hey influencers, listen to your audience! Retrieved from https://blog.intellifluence.com/hey-influencers-listen-to-your-audience-6eb59ebfee6c

[195] Lemkin, J. (2015, April 29). I hired my VP of marketing at $20k MRR. It wasn't a week too early. Retrieved from https://medium.com/@jasonlk/i-hired-my-vp-of-marketing-at-20k-mrr-it-wasn-t-a-week-too-early-74578470c758

[196] Dempsey, M. (2016, December 2). If you're not too early, you're too late. Retrieved from https://medium.com/@mhdempsey/if-youre-not-too-early-you-re-too-late-64f798229275

What the above process does is to help eliminate a lot of wasted time. There are millions of Pligg sites that are technically social networks. However, it is both unlikely that you're going to have 10 common friends that are using those accounts and equally unlikely that there will be anything novel about those networks — most exist for spam purposes. Even if you thought that one of those Pligg sites had 10 accounts worth following that you were connected to on Twitter and felt it was novel, would it be relevant to your niche? If you're a pet product influencer and 90 percent of the posts are about getting car insurance quotes and payday loans, the relevance isn't there. If by chance, you still felt it was close enough (dude, it isn't) the probability of having an account there translating into meaningful growth from non-bot accounts is low.

There are so many different networks out there that you need some sort of heuristic to keep you sane and engaging in the right places: focus[197].

Let's say you do manage to stumble onto something like a future VR-only network. For descriptive purposes, let's say it is like foursquare for VR. That approach is definitely novel, but until the network can manage to capture 10 of your common friends from other networks, it still won't be worth digging into. Why? Why wait? Most networks fail. This small filter helps you from wasting that time investment, and you most likely will be out nothing. Since you're an influencer who focuses on quality over quantity[198], this means you are posting on VR pet products at dog parks or whatever that intersection of niche and formatting is.

If you're in on a network at 1,000 users, it is mostly indistinguishable from being on a network at 10,000 (believe me, I've done it too many times). Additionally, let's say the heuristic kept you from joining the network until it was 100,000 strong—is that thinking such a bad thing? Chances are you'll still be one of the first handful of influencers within your niche using it as we suggest from previous articles. You're golden. Now you can rock this channel.

TIE YOUR ACCOUNTS

Once you manage to build an audience in that VR for foursquare-type idea, you need to be smart and bring it over to where you were previously applying the majority of your influence (probably Instagram and Pinterest?). From shoutouts to reminders to follow you elsewhere and linking all your social channels on all your profile pages, you need to cross promote. This point is what it is all about: growing your global audience as a means to expand individual network audiences.

---

[197] Sinkwitz, J. (2017, January 26). Becoming a top-tier influencer: Focus and authenticity. Retrieved from https://blog.intellifluence.com/becoming-a-top-tier-influencer-focus-and-authenticity-91b2ec154d0e

[198] Sinkwitz, J. (2017, February 27). Top-tier influencers: Quality over quantity. Retrieved from https://blog.intellifluence.com/top-tier-influencers-quality-over-quantity-e77662e74c79

Photo 26.1. Credit: DepositPhotos.com by mayoimages

CHAPTER 26

Go Offline to Win Online

There's more to networking than DMs and emails. Using online marketers as an example influencer niche, get a better understanding of why you should make yourself known in person and what type of events might make the most sense for you. Use the Should I Attend heuristic to quickly filter opportunities from distractions.

If you haven't guessed the theme of what matters by now in this half of the book on becoming a top-tier influencer[199], in addition to focusing on creating quality content[200] within one's chosen niche[201], it is vital to expand your visibility[202] by listening to your audience[203], being in the know[204], working with your community[205], performing outreach[206], and adopting newer social platforms[207] slightly earlier than your peers. Another technique that can set you apart involves a lot of hard work, and thus is overlooked: going offline.

GO OFFLINE

I don't mean unplugging and hanging out around the house taking a digital sabbatical, although there is also merit to that per Alex Soojung-Kim Pang PhD[208]. No, what I'm going to suggest is getting out and pressing fleshy palms with others in your market and in similar markets.

Nothing beats face-to-face interaction.

If you're always networking both online and offline, you'll be constantly expanding your web of both opportunities and growing your audience. If you recall to where we discussed the importance of co-citations as a means to imply expertise[209] when appearing next to other experts, the same is true of industry conference photos and blogger roundups. As easy as it is to dismiss them as cheesy, there's a reason why these particular pieces keep getting created: egobait increases content spread. When you are seen as a possible expert next to the other industry experts, the probability of getting a speaking engagement improves.

Rather than espouse the obvious benefits of mastering the art of simply showing up, let's instead look into some examples of where you might go. For this example, let's assume you're a mid-level online marketer based in the United States (there's a lot of you in our network — thank you!).

---

[199] Intellifluence (2016). Welcome, influencers. Retrieved from https://intellifluence.com/influencers

[200] Sinkwitz, J. (2017, February 27). Top-tier influencers: Quality over quantity. Retrieved from https://blog.intellifluence.com/top-tier-influencers-quality-over-quantity-e77662e74c79

[201] Sinkwitz, J. (2017, February 1). Optimize your influence. Retrieved from https://blog.intellifluence.com/optimize-your-influence-6720367fce0e

[202] Sinkwitz, J. (2017, January 17). Becoming a top-tier influencer: Get visible. Retrieved from https://blog.intellifluence.com/optimize-your-influence-6720367fce0e

[203] Sinkwitz, J. (2017, March 8). Hey influencers, listen to your audience! Retrieved from https://blog.intellifluence.com/hey-influencers-listen-to-your-audience-6eb59ebfee6c

[204] Sinkwitz, J. (2017, March 14). Be in the know, be first, be best. Retrieved from https://blog.intellifluence.com/be-in-the-know-be-first-or-be-best-d335f25771f4

[205] Sinkwitz, J. (2017, March 22). Community & collaboration. Retrieved from https://blog.intellifluence.com/community-collaboration-42ae57a1f2a0

[206] Sinkwitz, J. (2017, March 28). Influencer outreach, for influencers. Retrieved from https://blog.intellifluence.com/influencer-outreach-for-influencers-266frd4bfcafa

[207] Sinkwitz, J. (2017, April 7). Want hyper growth? Adopt early. Retrieved from https://blog.intellifluence.com/want-hyper-growth-adopt-early-ddcc67843da7

[208] Soojun-Kim Pang, A. (2014, July 19). Rules for a successful digital sabbatical. Retrieved from https://medium.com/contemplative-computing/rules-for-a-successful-digital-sabbath-5aafa445e883

[209] Sinkwitz, J. (2017, January 26). Becoming a top-tier influencer: Focus and authenticity. Retrieved from https://blog.intellifluence.com/becoming-a-top-tier-influencer-focus-and-authenticity-91b2ec154d0e

MEETUPS

Taking five minutes to Bing the answer (you heard me right Googlers) I found 2,414 different meetups[210] that could be potentially interesting to me in the realm of online marketing. There's just so many! Even if I select just those 25 miles from me, I get roughly 50 events that I can check out. This finding will be very handy later on with the heuristic on which events to attend. No matter your actual niche, there's almost certainly a meetup for it.

Photo 26.2. Credit: Pexels.com

CONFERENCES

There's no shortage of online marketing conferences as well; this list isn't exhaustive[211], but contains many that I've never heard of. Similar to meetups, there are many to choose from. I break these out slightly from meetups though for the purposes of size and scale—in my mind conferences are nothing but big meetups with an attendance fee.

SHOULD I ATTEND HEURISTIC

You can't be everywhere, despite your best efforts, so you need to try to maximize your offline efforts into those areas that can offer you the most significant growth. It isn't just about how big an event is though; you have to be as targeted on your attendance as you are with your content.

Audience Worth. First, you need to assign a value to increasing your audience size. There's a lot of ways to go about determining this value, and it really doesn't even matter what method you choose so long as you're consistent. For instance, GetApp suggests Twitter followers are worth more[212] than Facebook fans, but you could make your own determination on that. After you have a dollar figure attached to what your followers are worth, you can gauge how much expected growth is worth to you.

Value of Attending. Next, you need to have a rough understanding of the various people that will be attending the event. Mathematically figuring out how much growth you can get from interacting with someone is not exact; it's similar to how brands choose

[210] Meetup (2017). Online marketing. Retrieved from https://www.meetup.com/topics/online-marketing/us/
[211] Marketingterms.com (2017). 2017 digital marketing conferences, 300+ events worldwide (plus exclusive discounts). Retrieved from https://www.marketingterms.com/conferences/
[212] GetApp (2015, July 9). Why Twitter followers are worth more than Facebook fans. Retrieved from https://medium.com/@GetApp/why-twitter-followers-are-worth-more-than-facebook-fans-687f79c77772

influencers[213]. Relevance (as a percent) multiplied by Audience size multiplied by Engagement rate (as a percent) multiplied by Frequency of sharing for other influencers (as a percent) multiplied the probability of Getting Help (as a percent). It's guesswork mathematics! Keep in mind that you should be offering as much help as you're trying to receive; otherwise, your efforts are probably going to fall flat.

Cost to Attend. The important filter that comes into play next is the direct cost to attend: travel, lodging, attendance fees, etc. IF this cost exceeds (Value of Attending * Audience Worth), just stop right there and move on. You can try to stay in touch digitally, but if even on your best estimates the event exceeds what you're going to get out of it, don't go. This point is something I wish more people who attend every conference would ask themselves.

Opportunity Cost. This one is such an easy concept that most people seem to forget. Are there other events or activities that occur during the same time that would provide a greater value than this event? Put them through the same heuristic and simply go with the superior choice. In many cases, that might be the event you didn't expect, such as the online sellers group meetup with 150 people that takes place 10 miles from where you live .... It may not sound as appealing as going to the big flashy conference with numerous after-parties, but if you're serious about fixating on audience growth, go for cold hard math rather than what is hip and sexy. Remember, money is sexy.

JOE'S CONFERENCES

Your goal should be the ability to meet with people that have the biggest capacity to move your audience forward. For example, I attend SEOktoberfest every year. It isn't a big event, but it passes my heuristic easily. Why? The Value of Attending is significantly high because the entirety of the audience is at a level capable of changing each other's business overnight. Even though it takes place in Munich during a tourist heavy time, it consistently passes my heuristic.

Another event, Ungagged, also passes my heuristic, even though the audience mixture is somewhat different. The pricing, locale, and expected meetings are such that it offers a very good value, compared to what always seems to be a competing interest for my time. In its case, I was able to meet Rob Adler in person, whom not so coincidentally will be running our affiliate program on his Offer Stream Digital network in the next month or so.

I'll be polite and not list those conferences that wouldn't make my list. Instead, we can just focus on an extreme example. Is there value in me attending an intro to SEO meetup with 10 new college grads in Mozambique? As much as I like teaching and helping people grow their careers, the costs of the trip would almost certainly outweigh the rewards, especially when compared to other competitions for my time—there can absolutely be diamonds in

---

[213] Sinkwitz, J (2016, October 26). Time to pick the right product influencers. Retrieved from https://blog.intellifluence.com/time-to-pick-the-right-product-influencers-531c13ed49a1

the rough, and maybe I always wanted to travel to the African coast, but for the purposes of this heuristic, it wouldn't make the cut from a cost value alone.

Now, let's say my trip was subsidized, as often happens for speakers. If it were occurring in September or November, I'd still have to decline because the opportunity cost of missing out on my two favorite conferences would exceed the value gained from being at this faraway conference.

If you're serious about getting better at your influencing craft and want to grow your audience, there's no excuse to not attend at least a couple of events a year, especially if they're in your backyard. Do it and your path to becoming a top-tier influencer will get all that much clearer.

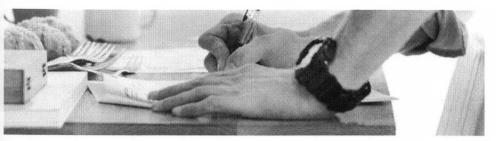

Photo 27.1. Credit: rawpixel.com

CHAPTER 27

Become an Authoritative Writer

One of the fastest ways to be viewed in your community as an expert is to become a published author; it's one of the reasons this guide even exists. Learn how to get yourself motivated, organized, and on track to publish your first book, as well as the importance of promoting the book.

Trying to build up your expertise? As you're offline at conferences[214] and meeting those in your community[215] who command speaking slots, have you noticed anything about the majority of them? They write. The reality is that authors are sought after for the best interviews, speaking slots, and media offers, which of course leads to the best product sponsorships (that is, the goal of many top-tier influencers[216]).

Telling you to become an authoritative writer is easier than actually becoming one, so let's start from scratch and walk through the process from never having written to self-publishing your first book. I'll try to do this part in under 1,000 words so you can focus on the actionable and less on the puffery that this topic usually attracts.

GETTING STARTED

The trite advice on how to get started writing is to just get started writing. Thankfully Mike Troiano is a bit more detailed in his post on getting started writing online[217]. At this point, you should already understand the "why" behind writing for the purpose of both improving visibility[218] as well as becoming an authority, so from his article, let's look at his "how"—as you can see, most of the important process for him is brainstorming and saving those as drafts, editing them after a day, kicking them around to others for feedback, and then incorporating that feedback over time as he mulls over a post.

Note that not all the processes are the same. For instance, I created a list of 29 topics related to influencer marketing, worked on sorting them into an outline with one- to two-sentence descriptions of what the articles would be about, and then, each week, I did a sprint to build out an article from title to final draft. Thankfully, I have a good editor in Andrew to make sure I don't come off as too much of an idiot (sorry, Joe, yes you do). Damnit Andrew!

Editor's note: That was all Joe; I didn't do it. I swear.

My process therefore is actually more similar to Jeff Goins and how he goes about writing novels[219]. He starts with the rough story idea, has it roughly outlined, backed with appropriate research and study, and only then fills in those gaps to complete the story. This process is the process that works for me, but you may find that Mike's approach works a bit better for you.

---

[214] Sinkwitz, J. (2017, April 11). Go offline to win online. Retrieved from https://blog.intellifluence.com/go-offline-to-win-online-7ca4091514d1

[215] Sinkwitz, J. (2017, March 22). Community & collaboration. Retrieved from https://blog.intellifluence.com/community-collaboration-42ae57a1f2a0

[216] Intellifluence (2016). Welcome, influencers. Retrieved from https://intellifluence.com/influencers

[217] Troiano, M. (2016, May 11). How do you start writing online? Retrieved from https://byrslf.co/how-do-you-start-writing-online-9a6fb3ef1f8a?gi=8e5a3624e40e

[218] Sinkwitz, J. (2017, January 17). Becoming a top-tier influencer: Get visible. Retrieved from https://blog.intellifluence.com/becoming-a-top-tier-influencer-get-visible-c8286796392e

[219] Goins, J (2016, November 18). Start writing a novel without having a clue what to do. Retrieved from https://medium.com/@jeffgoins/start-writing-a-novel-without-having-a-clue-what-to-do-2f2906279336

TOOLS TO KEEP YOU MOVING

After you get started writing and are knee-deep in the sludge of prepositions, Oxford commas, and ... ellipses, you might need some tools to keep you organized and push you toward the finish line.

1. Editorial planning, research, and the basics. CloudPeeps compiled a solid list[220] of a variety of tools. You'd be amazed how much can be accomplished with the right research and grammar checkers when it comes to organized writing and meeting deadlines.

2. Productivity. Pet peeve: life hacks for aspects of my life that don't require hacking. However, Chris Danilo has a list of some tools[221] I definitely agree with, when it comes to simply keeping you focused on putting the words on paper rather than refreshing Facebook. ToDoist and Evernote alone can keep you really focused. I couldn't get the meditation tools to work on me, but maybe they'll help you more.

3. Market your work. As Copypress says[222]: Like all forms of content, if you're creating your masterpiece in a vacuum, no one will know about it. Get it shared out, tell people what you're working on, brand yourself alongside the writing you're producing, and collect your best work for compiling into that major authoritative piece.

PUBLISH THAT BOOK

This is the stage I'm at, as an FYI. After this chapter is in the can and I get through the next two topics, I'll be able to provide a comprehensive guide on becoming a top-tier influencer, and then pair it with my previous guide[223]

to create a book. As an aside, I'm also going to promote it primarily via Intellifluence. How is that for dogfooding?!

Photo 27.2. Credit: Caio

[220] CloudPeeps (2015, August 11). 50 tools every freelance writer needs—from accounting to publishing. Retrieved from https://medium.com/@cloudpeeps/50-tools-every-freelance-writer-needs-from-accounting-to-publishing-a07e742ef338

[221] Danilo, C. (2015, July 25). 24 life changing productivity tools. Retrieved from https://medium.com/personal-growth/24-life-changing-productivity-tools-918306e1d876

[222] Mitchell, M. (2016, December 16). Creative spotlight: 6 ways to market yourself as a freelance writer. Retrieved from http://www.copypress.com/blog/6-ways-market-freelance-writer/

[223] Sinkwitz, J. (2017, January 5). The ultimate guide to using influencer marketing. Retrieved from https://blog.intellifluence.com/the-ultimate-guide-to-using-influencer-marketing-69021bae4b06

Let's talk about your book though. I'm still working on my first, but Yann Girard[224] has cranked out nine books as of March 2017. Much of his advice is similar to what we suggest throughout our blog on constant promotion and audience growth. The same was true of Poornima Vijayashanker on her self-publishing experiments[225]. There's really no magic to formatting and selling on Amazon. I just want to point to these two pieces so you understand how vital promotion is to getting success with the book, which, of course, leads back to the beginning of our journey on leveraging the published material as a means to gain authoritative status in your niche. If you need additional details on how to specifically self-publish on Amazon[226], Paul Jarvis has written a monster article on how to do it—yes, I did it again, because he also speaks to the absolute importance of promoting it.

OR PODCAST?

If writing isn't for you, the same appeal to authority can be found by hosting a niche podcast, interviewing other niche experts. This approach is exactly what the PositivePhil Podcast does, interviewing a wide variety of experts, which also helps to satisfy the going offline for networking purposes component to audience building—the man is always hustling! This approach can provide the same allure as an author, because if you remember back to the co-citation importance of authority, his constant airtime with other positive and powerful individuals gives him that similar allure.

Whether you decide to focus your words onto paper or into a microphone, when it comes to building up authority, there's no better way over that 10,000-hour[227] "becoming an expert" period to actually show off your expertise. It takes time and effort to be seen as an industry expert, but by focusing on the above approach, any influencer with a desire to succeed can make it happen.

[224] Girard, Y. (2017, March 18). What I learned self publishing 9 books (is self publishing dead)? Retrieved from https://medium.com/thought-pills/what-i-learned-self-publishing-9-books-is-self-publishing-dead-b2a78e59dd74
[225] Vijayashanker, P. (2015, October 27). Self-publishing: A series of experiments + endless self-promotion. Retrieved from https://artplusmarketing.com/self-publishing-a-series-of-experiments-endless-self-promotion-7890e659d3ba
[226] Jarvis, P. (2016, October 31). How to self-publish a non-fiction book on Amazon and make money. Retrieved from https://medium.com/nonfiction-self-publishing/how-to-self-publish-a-non-fiction-book-on-amazon-and-make-money-dfa49564b801
[227] Sinkwitz, J. (2017, February 21). The importance of influencer resilience. Retrieved from https://blog.intellifluence.com/the-importance-of-influencer-resilience-cd48ad5aca3b

Photo 28.1. Credit: DepositPhotos.com by nuchylee

CHAPTER 28

SPA Day — Syndicate. Promote. Amplify.

Your work cannot exist in a vacuum. Learn the basics of syndication, promotion, and amplification and how they can help you to improve the size of your audience.

If there's one thing I want to get across to you on this piece it is this: Great content cannot exist in a vacuum. When I was Chief of Revenue for CopyPress, this phrase was a constant pitch I'd make to organizations that were spending good money creating some really interesting material, but weren't investing in budget nor process when it came to ensuring that content was seen.

At this point, I'm going to assume you have selected a focus[228]; are pushing through the dips[229] while focusing on the quality[230] of your work; have an angle on being first, in the know, or the best; are listening to your audience[231]; and are working with your niche community[232]. That's all really necessary. I'm even going to assume that you're doing at least a little bit of offline networking[233] and working on becoming an authoritative writer[234], which leads to the next and maybe most important part: Promote yourself!

There are a lot of posts written on inbound marketing, but as Nichole Elizabeth DeMeré[235] explains, it isn't enough. Granted, she's discussing the concept from the perspective of SaaS businesses seeking growth, but that's even more of a reason to pay attention. Putting on my hat of having been in digital marketing for 20 years, most of what I read on inbound marketing is fluff that is meant for Fortune 500s with existing traffic flows —don't get me wrong, there's absolutely value in having your channels set up in ways to maximize flow of traffic to make use of it, but inbound DOES NOT exist without external effort. Anyone telling you otherwise is selling something. It reminds me of one of my wife's favorite movies ....

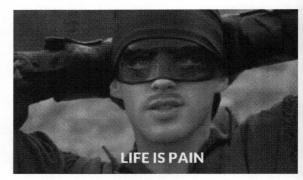

I'm not just using that because being married to me is painful; it probably is. I bring this up to get past the uncomfortable truth that no one will see your masterpiece

Graphic 28.1. Memes.com

[228] Sinkwitz, J. (2017, January 26). Becoming a top-tier influencer: Focus and authenticity. Retrieved from https://blog.intellifluence.com/becoming-a-top-tier-influencer-focus-and-authenticity-91b2ec154d0e

[229] Sinkwitz, J. (2017, February 21). The importance of influencer resilience. Retrieved from https://blog.intellifluence.com/the-importance-of-influencer-resilience-cd48ad5aca3b

[230] Sinkwitz, J. (2017, February 27). Top-tier influencers: Quality over quantity. Retrieved from https://blog.intellifluence.com/top-tier-influencers-quality-over-quantity-e77662e74c79

[231] Sinkwitz, J. (2017, March 8). Hey influencers, listen to your audience! Retrieved from https://blog.intellifluence.com/hey-influencers-listen-to-your-audience-6eb59ebfee6c

[232] Sinkwitz, J. (2017, March 22). Community & collaboration. Retrieved from https://blog.intellifluence.com/community-collaboration-42ae57a1f2a0

[233] Sinkwitz, J. (2017, April 11). Go offline to win online. Retrieved from https://blog.intellifluence.com/go-offline-to-win-online-7ca4091514d1

[234] Sinkwitz, J. (2017, April 19). Become an authoritative writer. Retrieved from https://blog.intellifluence.com/become-an-authoritative-writer-36e7a82914b3

[235] DeMeré, N. E. (2016, January 20). Inbound marketing alone isn't sufficient for SaaS customer success. Retrieved from https://medium.com/customer-s-success/inbound-marketing-alone-isn-t-sufficient-for-saas-customer-success-e728a5462987

unless you put in the effort to ensure it is seen. Let's go through some of the basics. Instead of the ABCs, we'll head to the SPA to Syndicate. Promote. Amplify.

SIMPLE SYNDICATION

One of the easiest things you can do is start syndicating your content. Having the brilliant blog post you just wrote auto-tweet out isn't exactly what I have in mind, though that's absolutely a step in the right direction. Using a tool like IFTTT (no relation to me), you could do so much more. Yes, not only could you have your blog posts auto-tweet and auto-Facebook post, but then you could have your Instagram channel post an image of the post a day later, then have that post auto-tweeted, then post your blog post on LinkedIn. This arrangement is just an example of simple syndication, and it is something every aspiring influencer[236] can do. If you have multiple channels, connect them. Professional burrito maker Justin Jackson[237] shares his own very simple syndication, which we'll touch on a bit later as it is similar to how my approach works.

COMPLEX SYNDICATION

A little bit trickier is complex syndication, because it involves you really working with your niche community and external partners. As an example, some period of time after this post goes live it'll eventually make its way over to Upwork—here's one from the influencer marketing guide[238] that I wrote for brands. This activity did not magically happen; I've been working with the Upwork team for several years on a variety of projects, so when the opportunity came up to getting my content syndicated to them, I jumped on it. Complex syndication is one way that the best influencers can separate themselves from the pack. This area is also where you can be rather creative in terms of where the syndication takes place.

Here's what will happen after this post goes live, just as far as syndication is concerned.

1. Auto-tweet to my personal audience

2. Auto-Facebook share to my personal audience

3. Posted onto company Twitter account

4. Posted onto company Facebook account

5. Submitted to Stumbleupon

6. Submitted to Hacker News

[236] Intellifluence (2016). Welcome, influencers. Retrieved from https://intellifluence.com/influencers

[237] Jackson, J. (2016, August 20). I generally syndicate content this way. Retrieved from https://medium.com/@mijustin/i-generally-syndicate-content-this-way-a77f1bfe9b7a

[238] Sinkwitz, J. (n.d.). Post-mortem: Why we test. Retrieved from https://www.upwork.com/hiring/for-clients/post-mortem-why-we-test/

7. Submitted to Inbound.org (yeah, aware of the irony here)

8. Submitted to Growthhackers

9. Contributed to a relevant Reddit sub

10. Reposted on my personal LinkedIn account

11. Used as an answer on Quora

12. Syndicated to Upwork

Of those steps on our straightforward syndication process, only step #12 might be difficult for you to copy, but even still I bet you could. If we pushed harder, could we contribute more into various search engine and marketing publications? Yes, and here's the awesome part of this bit—you can always layer on syndication later. For instance, after I turn this nine-month writing experiment into a book, it'll make even more sense for us to drip out syndicated articles through those channels, with a link to the book. Complex syndication isn't used enough to capture audiences.

PROMOTION

Syndication slips into promotion. The way I'm defining them, syndication is more of an initial process and promotion is a follow-on activity. So what do I mean then by promotion?

Outreach is one such method. Jay does this with bloggers[239] to both promote existing content as well as to build links (which, of course, has direct traffic and search benefits). Outreach is not easy; you know this point because we wrote about outreach already[240].

Another method is what I'd probably call syndication++ (nerd joke). James Carbary covers it on his post for promoting content like a boss[241] wherein you aren't just syndicating your content but instead are repeatedly doing so with In Case You Missed It (ICYMI)-styled posts. The reason this piece should be part of your toolkit is because not only is it easy to set up and schedule at defined intervals, but also because you can't predict when your audiences are going to be both in front of your material AND in the right mindset to engage with it. It allows you to get multiple chances.

AMPLIFICATION

The next step from simple promotion is what some of us refer to as amplification. Some

[239] Jay. (2017, February 27). How we use blogger outreach to promote content and build links. Retrieved from https://medium.com/@Jay52/how-we-use-blogger-outreach-to-promote-content-and-build-links-643564d1dcb7
[240] Sinkwitz, J. (2017, March 28). Influencer outreach, for influencers. Retrieved from https://blog.intellifluence.com/influencer-outreach-for-influencers-266fd4bfcafa
[241] Carbary, J. (2016, March 30). How to promote your content like a boss. Retrieved from https://medium.com/@jamescarbary/how-to-promote-your-content-like-a-boss-d78bb87b41c3

brands using Intellifluence[242] use it primarily for amplification purposes. Who knew? I think Warren Knight would approve, as using thought leaders and industry influencers is part of his amplification process[243] as well.

I'd like to save some keystrokes here because amplification to me leads to discussing compulsion marketing[244], which might be a bit heavy for a single influencer's purpose. If you're really into learning about that topic, you can read about brand amplification here[245].

If you didn't click through to read the more in-depth compulsion marketing concepts, let's cover some basics that make more sense for the indie influencer:

1. Pay other influencers. That's right, and it absolutely works. You can think of this idea as incented community interaction. As you're still working your way up to being one of the top dogs (or cats, if you're a cat person), you will probably need to provide some sort of compensation in order to get amplification from your niche community. Yes, this means paying to have your posts retweeted, shared, etc., but it can also mean you could assist on their collaboration projects in exchange for their efforts. That's the beauty of such exchanges. You can get a lot accomplished without paying much out of pocket if you exchange with in-kind work.

2. Native ad networks—I know some really smart marketers that get their material seen via AdWords, where their KPI is actually links earned by hyper-focused campaigns. Others have taken that approach and applied it to Facebook, where you can amplify your posts for pennies. Then, there's native ad traffic, which can deliver a ridiculous amount of cheap traffic that exists off-platform and bring it to you on your personal assets. To keep it simple, if you are looking to amplify a Facebook post, use Facebook's ad platform. If you are looking to amplify a tweet, use Twitter's ad platform. If you are looking to promote your blog, use a native ad network.

3. Email—This topic is so big that it is the next chapter in this series. Thus, I'll just say that if you aren't collecting emails, start yesterday. We'll cover this topic in significantly more depth.

There you have it. After a hard week of creating some stellar content, treat yourself to a SPA day to setup your syndication, promotion, and amplification processes.

[242] Intellifluence (2016). Hello, brands. Retrieved from https://intellifluence.com/brands
[243] Knight, W. (2016, February 11). How to amplify your content to your target audiences and generate leads. Retrieved from https://medium.com/@WarrenKnight/how-to-amplify-your-content-to-your-target-audience-and-generate-leads-8f9aa728a76d
[244] Intellifluence (2016). Compulsion marketing: Making your campaign irresistible. Retrieved from https://www.slideshare.net/intellifluence/compulsion-marketing-making-your-campaign-irresistible
[245] Sinkwitz, J. (2016, December 7). How to maximize exposure on your product reviews. Retrieved from https://blog.intellifluence.com/how-to-maximize-exposure-on-your-product-reviews-23336c3492a4

Photo 29.1. Credit: rawpixel.com

CHAPTER 29

Build That Email List

One of the most resilient forms of marketing and income generation is still email. Learn why you need to be maintaining an email list, how to build the list, and what type of value your audience members expect in exchange for giving you their email addresses.

My dear influencer, you are nearly there. If there's one last thing I could implore you to do, it is this: Build that email list!

It is one thing to have followers, but another thing entirely to have fans, and fans are likely to give you their email addresses. Why should you care? I would argue that having a healthy email list is more important than catching a trending social network[246] or becoming an author[247], in terms of continual impact. Those connections can be very valuable to you as well.

WHY SHOULD YOU BUILD AN EMAIL LIST?

1. Email will likely still be around when that next hot social network is sold for pennies on the dollar to Facegoog. The present is littered with the forgotten rocket ships of the past, and by the past, I mean even a few months ago. Still doing Periscope videos? I do them as often as I update my Geocities page. Don't just take my word on this point; Michael K. Spencer goes into detail about how social networks fail[248], using Peach as an example. Email existed before all the social networks you use, and it may exist after all of them disappear.

2. Email allows you a very direct connection to your audience, without a lot of prying eyes. Want to provide some personal touches to go with that exclusivity? This process is how. If you are as authentic as Ryan Hoover is with his list, you can make that happen. Note in his very first bullet point on his email list data[249] that being personal is exceedingly important.

3. Poornima Vijayashanker argues in her heuristic on receiving and processing feedback[250] the importance of credibility, closeness, and key audience when it comes to even processing that feedback (and you know how I love heuristics!). If that feedback is coming via your solicitation of your fans, that feedback ticks off all those heuristic filters. Further, it isn't blindsided feedback either, which is even better since you'll be in an ideal position to process and act on it.

4. Need to amplify a post[251]? You can make a direct appeal to those most likely to help you out. Remember that even with proper syndication and scheduling your posts may get lost in the shuffle of everyone else's posts, even to an audience that loves you. Sending out recap emails and strong suggestions to read will have a profound

[246] Sinkwitz, J. (2017, April 7). Want hyper growth? Adopt early. Retrieved from https://blog.intellifluence.com/want-hyper-growth-adopt-early-ddcc67843da7

[247] Sinkwitz, J. (2017, April 19). Becoming an authoritative writer. Retrieved from https://blog.intellifluence.com/become-an-authoritative-writer-36e7a82914b3

[248] Spencer, M. K. (2016, January 10). Peach social network — how social media fails. Retrieved from https://medium.com/@Michael_Spencer/peach-social-network-how-social-media-fails-12e9e40261ba

[249] Hoover, R. (2013, July 7). My email list: 58% open rate, 23% CTR. Retrieved from https://medium.com/@rrhoover/my-email-list-58-open-rate-23-ctr-1a453c2cca98

[250] Vijayashanker, P. (2016, June 2). Feedback got you in a frenzy? Learn how to filter it. Retrieved from https://medium.com/@poornima/feedback-got-you-in-a-frenzy-learn-how-to-filter-it-4ee1ef5e0d99

[251] Sinkwitz, J. (2017, April 24). SPA Day — Syndicate. Promote. Amplify.

effect on those amplification efforts. Just don't abuse this approach. If you have a light touch recap on your reviews, they can be useful, but save the urgency and direct appeals to only those most important posts.

HOW DO YOU BUILD AN EMAIL LIST?

There are a few different ways to build lists, meaning there's not one right way to do it. Therefore, I'd like to provide some options for you, depending on what type of influencer[252] you are.

Blogs. Some of the simplest advice I've come across is from James Carbary, where he outlines the six-step process[253] he uses as a blogger to build a list. Right off the bat, he focuses on the importance of creating that quality content[254], which I naturally agree with. His approach is good because for the most part it is not "in your face." It guides readers that are interested in the content or additional offers multiple opportunities to sign up. I especially like his note on pop-up call to actions (CTAs). The importance of the call to action when asking for that email might be one of the most important email acquisition techniques. My favorite neuromarketer Roger Dooley shares some examples from top conversion experts[255] worth checking out (stealing) as you go about getting your existing base to convert over into your burgeoning email list.

Instagram. Unless my stats at Intellifluence lie, you're my biggest group of users at the moment. Let's follow the steps already outlined by Sleeknote on turning Instagram followers into email subscribers[256]. The most important consideration is to make sure your website URL is on your profile. Make it specific for your user base so they know they're getting something special. In other words, if you have a discount code, don't just list the code on your profile or in a post, but instead direct the audience to go to the website to get it. Once you get the users to your website, use the CTA advice for bloggers above, so you can convert them to your email list. The rest of the advice is a bit more obvious to influencers. Creating stunning imagery is all part of the job description.

Facebook. According to Julia Jornsay-Silverberg, it is all about your goals. Know that you want emails more than likes, and then act on that want. What's neat about her advice on using Facebook to grow your email list[257] is that you can absolutely incorporate it into your current Facebook posting process and use the promoted post option. In this scenario, your

[252] Intellifluence (2016). Welcome, influencers. Retrieved from https://intellifluence.com/influencers
[253] Carbary, J. (2016, April 1). How to build an email list with your blog (a six-step process). Retrieved from https://medium.com/@jamescarbary/how-to-build-an-email-list-with-your-blog-a-6-step-process-c8c5cdef0cda
[254] Sinkwitz, J. (2017, February 27). Top-tier influencers: Quality over quantity. Retrieved from https://blog.intellifluence.com/top-tier-influencers-quality-over-quantity-e77662e74c79
[255] Dooley, R. (2015, March 31). How the world's top conversion experts seduce you into giving up your email. Retrieved from https://medium.com/@rogerdooley/how-the-world-s-top-conversion-experts-seduce-you-into-giving-up-your-email-84922530f8eb
[256] Sleeknote (2017, March 14). A beginner's guide to turning Instagram followers into subscribers. Retrieved from https://medium.com/sleeknotes-e-commerce-favorites/a-beginners-guide-to-turning-instagram-followers-into-subscribers-158412468c72
[257] Jornay-Silverberg (2016, January 4). How to use Facebook to grow your email list. Retrieved from https://medium.com/@jbethjs/how-to-use-facebook-to-grow-your-email-list-f719ea01bbfb

posts that had the best email sign-up rates can be co-opted as ads.

LinkedIn. A lot of the above advice applies to you, although we're taking a more professional angle. As a reminder to everyone, LinkedIn is NOT and SHOULD NOT be Facebook. [/rant] Chris Spurvey built his email list primary on LinkedIn[258], which will look pretty similar to the approaches taken by bloggers. It is all about the compelling content with hooks for more compelling content and extras. Again, like blogs and a concept used throughout, the use of large CTAs and lead magnets such as the exclusive content giveaway works rather well.

Twitter. See the advice for Facebook. Really, the only change here is that you're selecting a post in Twitter's ad interface to promote vs. in Facebook's ad interface. Otherwise, the advice is identical.

Pinterest. See Instagram. There are slight nuances, such as where you would provide a URL for email signups, but otherwise, the above advice is sufficient.

Photo 29.2. Credit: Pexels.com

WHY WOULD YOUR AUDIENCE WANT TO JOIN THE LIST?

Now, there could be a variety of reasons why someone might give you an email address, but it generally boils down to value and access. Think through each reason why a person might want to join your list and you'll be able to tailor your pitch to that reason:

1. Discounts and Special Offers (Value). If this area is the main reason someone wants to join your list, then you can entice and keep them simply by continuing to provide regular discounts. I would caution you to act more like AppSumo than Groupon though—be focused and remain authentic[259].

2. Exclusive Content (Knowledge). Similar to discounts and special offers, you can tailor your CTAs to this type of offer and then deliver on it. What's different is that discounts are somewhat simpler to create future instances of. To keep an audience that craves special content happy, you need to keep creating exclusive content, but you can also use that desire to your advantage by requiring a series of steps in order to get that content.

[258] Spurvey, C. (2016, December 23). How I grew my email list using LinkedIn (and now Medium). Retrieved from https://medium.com/your-brand/how-i-grew-my-email-list-using-linkedin-and-now-medium-9e8985e0477b

[259] Sinkwitz, J. (2017, January 26). Becoming a top-tier influencer: Focus and authenticity. Retrieved from https://blog.intellifluence.com/becoming-a-top-tier-influencer-focus-and-authenticity-91b2ec154d0e

3. Access (Belonging). The access I'm referring to is more about community[260] than physical access. I will periodically sign up to certain comedians' email lists. It isn't just so I can sniff a sweater they left behind after a show, wear it, and adopt their identity while I talk to my pets, alone, in the dark. No, this access is about knowing when special "insider-only" events are occurring, what might be coming next out of the community, etc. Not the creepy kind of access.

By knowing what your audience wants, you can best create an offer to ensure you can capture those email addresses and build up a more bulletproof audience as you complete your journey on becoming a top-tier influencer.

There you have it. I've provided a set of tools that, when used correctly, can help a person fresh to a social network grow to respectable size and income using influencer marketing. I've armed you as best I can and now the rest is up to you. Peer-level influencer marketing works, and you can be a part of it[261]. When I started my two guides for how to use influencer marketing and this one on becoming a top-tier influencer, we at Intellifluence didn't have a very large reach.

And now? As of this writing, the numbers are already outdated due to a constant flow of influencer signups. But stew on this: In aggregate, our reach is now bigger than Kim Kardashian ... just by connecting with ordinary individuals every day for nine months.

Know what is crazier? Now that this material has been published in a book, at the close of 2017, we believe our reach will be 3 times to more than 10 times greater than our current reach. Agencies and brands[262] cannot ignore the power of peers and what they bring, nor the risk mitigation provided. This environment is good for you, it is good for me, and it is good for them. Expect a wild ride in the next couple of years because influencer marketing isn't going away. I hope you end up riding along with us.

Editor's note: Dec 2017 was 10x previously discussed reach.

[260] Sinkwitz, J. (2017, March 22). Community & collaboration. Retrieved from https://blog.intellifluence.com/community-collaboration-42ae57a1f2a0

[261] Intellifluence (2016). Welcome, influencers. Retrieved from https://intellifluence.com/influencers

[262] Intellifluence (2016). Hello, brands. Retrieved from https://intellifluence.com/brands

EPILOGUE

Dave and I can't stress enough just how fast the marketing world is moving toward influencer marketing. We've both been around the block a couple of decades each, having seen a wide variety of tactics come and go, but the concept discussed for brands, agencies, and individuals transcends any specific medium. People trust people, especially those they know and already have a connection with.

Think through your past several years of purchasing and ask yourself the following questions:

When you were shopping for a car, did you rely on a car commercial you saw? A banner ad? An email? Or, did you rely on some very specific information, whether it be a friend who knows a lot about cars, a forum discussion on cars, or perhaps even an article written by a well-known and respected car reviewer?

After buying that car, you're driving to work where you know you need to address a very important problem of picking a new CRM for the company. You have several brochures on your desk from a recent tradeshow, but is that how you'll choose? Every day your inbox has been hit with a couple of those reps, but thus far it is just attempts to get you on the phone and read from a canned script. Then there's your friend Gary who recently tweeted out his love for the CRM his company uses, and that guy is a pro – so which would you trust more in the purchasing decision?

Time to celebrate for picking the right CRM and getting that promotion! You're sitting down to order dinner at a nice restaurant with your significant other. When choosing a wine, do you lean more toward that which has a prettier label or the sommelier's suggestions after having attempted to assess your palate? I really hope you're in the latter camp rather than the former.

The broadcast mediums such as television, radio, and cold email aren't going to disappear, but their role is changing significantly to act as top-of-funnel channels, with lead nurturing and assisted closing of a sale happening more due to influencers ...whether or not you previously recognized those individuals as having influenced you, or whether you recognize they are paid or organically providing that influence. As individuals begin to understand their niche relevance, expect more self-organization to occur, making it easier to seek out topical experts, bypassing what is currently a very noisy online world competing for your attention. Don't be left behind.

REFERENCES

Barker, S. (2016, March 10). 5 reasons why influencer marketing shouldn't be ignored. Retrieved from https://socialmediaweek.org/blog/2016/03/5-reasons-influencer-marketing-shouldnt-ignored/

Blake, R. (2017, January 16). Can you really be everywhere at once in #socialmedia? Retrieved from https://medium.com/@robertoblake/can-you-really-be-everywhere-at-once-in-socialmedia-9c0500941117

Blank, S. (2017, February 3). VC's are not your friends, they're frenemies. Retrieved from https://medium.com/startup-grind/vcs-are-not-your-friends-they-re-frenemies-e3dacb9be631

Boostinsider (2016, October 21). What is product influencer fit? Retrieved from https://blog.boostinsider.com/what-is-product-influencer-fit-c2ef51d19b36?gi=a439db32dd12

Bowbrick, S. (2016, November 4). How is this only six seconds? Retrieved from https://medium.com/@bowbrick/how-is-this-only-six-seconds-a37cbcafab2a

Brand24 (2017, February 23). Google Alerts alternative. Retrieved from https://medium.com/@brand24/google-alerts-alternative-7505be30fa4c

Brown, D. (2015, March 16). Coopetition. Retrieved from https://medium.com/@brownorama/if-my-occasional-tweets-and-instagram-posts-about-it-haven-t-convinced-you-i-m-loving-joshua-wolf-ef138393968e

Bullas, J. (n.d.) 7 tips to become an influencer in your industry. Retrieved from http://www.jeffbullas.com/7-tips-become-influencer-industry/

Carbary, J. (2016, April 1). How to build an email list with your blog (a six-step process). Retrieved from https://medium.com/@jamescarbary/how-to-build-an-email-list-with-your-blog-a-6-step-process-c8c5cdef0cda

Carbary, J. (2016, March 30). How to promote your content like a boss. Retrieved from https://medium.com/@jamescarbary/how-to-promote-your-content-like-a-boss-d78bb87b41c3

Carmichael, E. (2015, September 24). "People's lives are a direct reflection of the expectations of their peer groups." Retrieved from https://medium.com/@EvanCarmichael/people-s-lives-are-a-direct-reflection-of-the-expectations-of-their-peer-group-e8de8327988a

Chaffey, D. (2017, April 6). How to define SMART marketing objectives. Retrieved from http://www.smartinsights.com/goal-setting-evaluation/goals-kpis/define-smart-marketing-objectives/

CloudPeeps (2015, August 11). 50 tools every freelance writer needs—from accounting to publishing. Retrieved from https://medium.com/@cloudpeeps/50-tools-every-freelance-writer-needs-from-accounting-to-publishing-a07e742ef338

Collins, J. (2015, October 15). Purposeful Pareto: 400 hours is all you need to become 'not half bad.' Retrieved from https://medium.com/@jonno/purposeful-pareto-400-hours-is-all-you-need-to-become-not-half-bad-896c6f4a0046

CopyPress (n.d.). Copywriting guide. Retrieved from http://community.copypress.com/guides/copywriting/the-basics/why-do-people-share-online-content/

Danilo, C. (2015, July 25). 24 life changing productivity tools. Retrieved from https://medium.com/personal-growth/24-life-changing-productivity-tools-918306e1d876

DeMeré, N. E. (2016, January 20). Inbound marketing alone isn't sufficient for SaaS customer success. Retrieved from https://medium.com/customer-s-success/inbound-marketing-alone-isn-t-sufficient-for-saas-customer-success-e728a5462987

Dempsey, M. (2016, December 2). If you're not too early, you're too late. Retrieved from https://medium.com/@mhdempsey/if-youre-not-too-early-you-re-too-late-64f798229275

DiVitto, A. (2016, September 11). 4 ways to use Facebook trending topics for your business. Retrieved from https://blog.markgrowth.com/4-ways-to-use-facebook-trending-topics-for-your-business-6086d63e9559

Dooley, R. (2015, March 31). How the world's top conversion experts seduce you into giving up your email. Retrieved from https://medium.com/@rogerdooley/how-the-world-s-top-conversion-experts-seduce-you-into-giving-up-your-email-84922530f8eb

Drish, A. (2016, January 7). The missing chapter of "the dip" every entrepreneur should know about. Retrieved from https://medium.com/hackerpreneur-magazine/the-missing-chapter-of-the-dip-every-entrepreneur-should-know-about-8942b4a3e934

Evans, A. (2016, September 15). The power of the peer influencer. Retrieved from https://blog.intellifluence.com/the-power-of-the-peer-influencer-6c7eaadbfa85

Federal Trade Commission (n.d.). Division of advertising practices. Retrieved from https://www.ftc.gov/about-ftc/bureaus-offices/bureau-consumer-protection/our-divisions/division-advertising-practices

FireDrum (n.d.). Full service email marketing pricing. Retrieved from https://www.firedrumemailmarketing.com/email-marketing-full-service-program/

Garcia, A. (2015, November 7). How this company earns millions with Instagram. Retrieved from http://money.cnn.com/2015/11/07/smallbusiness/frank-body-startup-coffee-scrub/index.html

GetApp (2015, July 9). Why Twitter followers are worth more than Facebook fans. Retrieved from https://medium.com/@GetApp/why-twitter-followers-are-worth-more-than-facebook-fans-687f79c77772

Girard, Y. (2017, March 18). What I learned self publishing 9 books (is self publishing dead)? Retrieved from https://medium.com/thought-pills/what-i-learned-self-publishing-9-books-is-self-publishing-dead-b2a78e59dd74

Goins, J. (2016, November 18). Start writing a novel without having a clue what to do. Retrieved from https://medium.com/@jeffgoins/start-writing-a-novel-without-having-a-clue-what-to-do-2f290627933b

Hakes, T. (n.d.). How we scaled a startup from 0 organic traffic to 100,000 visitors per month (in about one year). Retrieved from http://yesoptimist.com/content-marketing-seo-case-study-the-trifecta-strategy/

Haralambous, N. (2016, July 1). Find a niche, not a population. Retrieved from https://medium.com/found-it/find-a-niche-not-a-population-2a588bfe39f6

Hoover, R. (2013, July 7). My email list: 58% open rate, 23% CTR. Retrieved from https://medium.com/@rrhoover/my-email-list-58-open-rate-23-ctr-1a453c2cca98

Instagram Engineering (2015, July 6). Trending on Instagram. Retrieved from https://engineering.instagram.com/trending-on-instagram-b749450e6d93?gi=2de0f8d676d0

Intellifluence (2016). Ask us anything. Retrieved from https://intellifluence.com/contact

Intellifluence (2016). Brands, try us for free. Retrieved from https://intellifluence.com/register

Intellifluence (2016). Compulsion marketing: Making your campaign irresistible. Retrieved from https://www.slideshare.net/intellifluence/compulsion-marketing-making-your-campaign-irresistible

Intellifluence (2016). Create an influencer account. Retrieved from https://intellifluence.com/influencers/register

Intellifluence (2016). Find the right influencers and make more sales. Retrieved from https://intellifluence.com/discover?geo=all&network=all&category=all

Intellifluence (2016). Hello, brands. Retrieved from https://intellifluence.com/influencers/

Intellifluence. (2016). Our pricing is simple. Retrieved from https://intellifluence.com/pricing

Intellifluence (2016). Welcome, influencers. Retrieved from https://intellifluence.com/influencers/

Iuliano, A. (2016, October 29). How to go viral on every social media. Retrieved from https://medium.com/@AustinIuliano/how-to-go-viral-on-every-social-media-9ed589379ec8

Jackson, J. (2016, August 20). I generally syndicate content this way. Retrieved from https://medium.com/@mijustin/i-generally-syndicate-content-this-way-a77f1bfe9b7a

Jarvis, P. (2016, October 31). How to self-publish a non-fiction book on Amazon and make money. Retrieved from https://medium.com/nonfiction-self-publishing/how-to-self-publish-a-non-fiction-book-on-amazon-and-make-money-dfa49564b801

Jay. (2017, February 27). How we use blogger outreach to promote content and build links. Retrieved from https://medium.com/@Jay52/how-we-use-blogger-outreach-to-promote-content-and-build-links-643564d1dcb7

Jornay-Silverberg (2016, January 4). How to use Facebook to grow your email list. Retrieved from https://medium.com/@jbethjs/how-to-use-facebook-to-grow-your-email-list-f719ea01bbfb

Kemp, P. (2015, October 31). A crazy week getting noticed by the tech press. Retrieved from https://medium.com/@TheAppGuy/a-crazy-week-of-getting-noticed-by-the-tech-press-b113d6bb50df

Kim, L. (2017, January 19). 11 ways to hack the LinkedIn Pulse algorithm. Retrieved from https://medium.com/marketing-and-entrepreneurship/11-ways-to-hack-the-linkedin-pulse-algorithm-219813bf8b7b

Kleinberg, S. (2015, November 5). Twitter moments: There's no lightning. Retrieved from https://medium.com/@scottkleinberg/twitter-moments-there-s-no-lightning-6fbb786d9fe6

Knight, W. (2016, February 11). How to amplify your content to your target audiences and generate leads. Retrieved from https://medium.com/@WarrenKnight/how-to-amplify-your-content-to-your-target-audience-and-generate-leads-8f9aa728a76d

Know Your Meme (2014). Children's book cover parodies. Retrieved from http://knowyourmeme.com/memes/childrens-book-cover-parodies

Koenigs, M. (2016, June 23). How to find your niche (for your business or your book). Retrieved from https://medium.com/@MikeKoenigs/how-to-find-your-niche-for-your-business-or-your-book-f22db3104c79

Lee, K. (2016, August 29). How often to post to Facebook, Twitter, LinkedIn and more. Retrieved from https://stories.buffer.com/how-often-to-post-to-facebook-twitter-linkedin-and-more-bb2758459162

Lemkin, J. (2015, April 29). I hired my VP of marketing at $20k MRR. It wasn't a week too early. Retrieved from https://medium.com/@jasonlk/i-hired-my-vp-of-marketing-at-20k-mrr-it-wasn-t-a-week-too-early-74578470c758

Marketingterms.com (2017). 2017 digital marketing conferences, 300+ events worldwide (plus exclusive discounts). Retrieved from https://www.marketingterms.com/conferences/

McCaughey, B. (2017, March 9). A beginners guide to getting noticed. Retrieved from https://medium.com/@multitude27/a-beginners-guide-to-getting-noticed-76f5f8c4fc91

Meetup (2017). Online marketing. Retrieved from https://www.meetup.com/topics/online-marketing/us/

Mitchell, M. (2016, December 16). Creative spotlight: 6 ways to market yourself as a freelance writer. Retrieved from http://www.copypress.com/blog/6-ways-market-freelance-writer/

Ogle, S. (2016, September 13). 59 amazing tools to help you create remarkable content easily. Retrieved from https://medium.com/@seanogle/59-amazing-tools-to-help-you-create-remarkable-content-easily-f406f0ae3c99

Radice, R. (2016, November 11). 4 ways to leverage Facebook Live. Retrieved from https://medium.com/@RebekahRadice/4-ways-to-leverage-facebook-live-494b38223159

Rampton, J. (2015, September 24). How to guest blog anywhere. Retrieved from https://www.johnrampton.com/how-to-guest-post-anywhere/

Read, Ashley. (2016, July 14). The complete guide to Instagram marketing. Retrieved from https://stories.buffer.com/the-complete-guide-to-instagram-marketing-a0ff0711bdc1?gi=d866af17eff5

Rosenberg, S. (2015, May 8). Shut down your office. You now work in Slack. Retrieved from https://www.wired.

com/2015/05/shut-down-your-office-you-now-work-in-slack/

Scherck, J. (2016, October 18). 150+ of the best case study examples for B2B product marketers. Retrieved from https://www.docsend.com/best-b2b-case-study-examples/

Simms, M. (n.d.) Empowering authors. Retrieved from http://prinfluencers.com/10-weeks-to-media-mentions/

Sinkwitz, J. (2016, August 12). Why I left a $250K/year CMO position to found a startup. Retrieved from https://theascent.biz/why-i-left-a-250k-yr-cmo-position-to-found-a-startup-fd9f617a8319

Sinkwitz, J. (2016, August 15). How to influence your buyers using content marketing. Retrieved from http://www.copypress.com/blog/how-to-influence-buyers-using-content-marketing/

Sinkwitz, J. (2016, August 22). Content marketing playbook: Reflections on influencer marketing. Retrieved from https://lseo.com/influencer-marketing/

Sinkwitz, J. (2016, August 29). Optimizing for Product Hunt: How not to. Retrieved from https://theascent.biz/optimizing-for-product-hunt-how-not-to-74ed01a4e7a9

Sinkwitz, J. (2016, December 7). How to maximize exposure on your product reviews. Retrieved from https://blog.intellifluence.com/how-to-maximize-exposure-on-your-product-reviews-23336c3492a4

Sinkwitz, J. (2016, December 14). Round two: Use the same reviewers or get new ones? Retrieved from https://blog.intellifluence.com/round-two-use-the-same-reviewers-or-get-new-ones-8cc22e349bd0

Sinkwitz, J. (2016, November 22). So you got your first review; now what? Retrieved from https://blog.intellifluence.com/so-you-got-your-first-review-now-what-13df54960fbf

Sinkwitz, J. (2016, November 28). Influencer negotiation: What is fair? Retrieved from https://blog.intellifluence.com/influencer-negotiation-what-is-fair-20f05dac4234

Sinkwitz, J. (2016, October 3). Amazon: No more incentivized reviews*. Retrieved from https://blog.intellifluence.com/amazon-no-more-incentivized-reviews-d109ad66ad64

Sinkwitz, J. (2016, October 5). Who exactly are you trying to influence? Retrieved from https://blog.intellifluence.com/who-are-you-trying-to-influence-ba8ddaf5a575

Sinkwitz, J. (2016, October 11). Which social channel will bring sales for your business? Retrieved from https://blog.intellifluence.com/which-social-channel-will-bring-sales-for-your-business-c8831fb0c4e2

Sinkwitz, J. (2016, October 18). Determining the right influencer type for your campaign. Retrieved from https://blog.intellifluence.com/determining-the-right-influencer-type-for-your-campaign-837a8fe94ff2

Sinkwitz, J. (2016, October 26). Time to pick the right product influencers. Retrieved from https://blog.intellifluence.com/time-to-pick-the-right-product-influencers-531c13ed49a1

Sinkwitz, J. (2016, October 31). How to pitch influencers. Retrieved from https://blog.intellifluence.com/how-to-pitch-influencers-5b2dd319a0c6

Sinkwitz, J. (2016, September 13). What is influencer marketing? Retrieved from https://blog.intellifluence.com/what-is-influencer-marketing-40549fe706b4

Sinkwitz, J. (2016, September 19). Why should influencer marketing be a part of your strategy? Retrieved from https://blog.intellifluence.com/why-should-influencer-marketing-be-a-part-of-your-strategy-88122ece9dab

Sinkwitz, J. (2016, September 28). How to set goals for your influencer campaign. Retrieved from https://blog.intellifluence.com/how-to-set-goals-for-your-influencer-campaign-abc236257f79

Sinkwitz, J. (2017, April 7). Want hyper growth? Adopt early. Retrieved from https://blog.intellifluence.com/want-hyper-growth-adopt-early-ddcc67843da7

Sinkwitz, J. (2017, April 11). Go offline to win online. Retrieved from https://blog.intellifluence.com/go-offline-to-win-online-7ca4091514d1

Sinkwitz, J. (2017, April 19). Become an authoritative writer. Retrieved from https://blog.intellifluence.com/become-an-authoritative-writer-36e7a82914b3

Sinkwitz, J. (2017, April 24). SPA Day — Syndicate. Promote. Amplify.

Sinkwitz, J. (2017, February 1). Optimize your influence. Retrieved from https://blog.intellifluence.com/optimize-your-influence-6720367fce0e

Sinkwitz, J. (2017, February 8). Influencers should negotiate, too. Retrieved from https://blog.intellifluence.com/influencers-should-negotiate-too-22490d1014f1

Sinkwitz, J. (2017, February 21). The importance of influencer resilience. Retrieved from https://blog.intellifluence.com/the-importance-of-influencer-resilience-cd48ad5aca3b

Sinkwitz, J. (2017, February 27). Top-tier influencers: Quality over quantity. Retrieved from https://blog.intellifluence.com/top-tier-influencers-quality-over-quantity-e77662e74c79

Sinkwitz, J. (2017, January 5). The ultimate guide to using influencer marketing. Retrieved from https://blog.intellifluence.com/the-ultimate-guide-to-using-influencer-marketing-69021bae4b06

Sinkwitz, J. (2017, January 17). Become a top-tier influencer. Retrieved from https://blog.intellifluence.com/becoming-a-top-tier-influencer-get-visible-c8286796392e

Sinkwitz, J. (2017, January 26). Becoming a top-tier influencer: Focus and authenticity. Retrieved from https://blog.intellifluence.com/becoming-a-top-tier-influencer-focus-and-authenticity-91b2ec154d0e

Sinkwitz, J. (2017, March 8). Hey influencers, listen to your audience! Retrieved from https://blog.intellifluence.com/hey-influencers-listen-to-your-audience-6eb59ebfee6c

Sinkwitz, J. (2017, March 14). Be in the know, be first, be best. Retrieved from https://blog.intellifluence.com/be-in-the-know-be-first-or-be-best-d335f25771f4

Sinkwitz, J. (2017, March 22). Community & collaboration. Retrieved from https://blog.intellifluence.com/community-collaboration-42ae57a1f2a0

Sinkwitz, J. (2017, March 28). Influencer outreach, for influencers. Retrieved from https://blog.intellifluence.com/influencer-outreach-for-influencers-266fd4bfcafa

Sinkwitz, J. (n.d.). Post-mortem: Why we test. Retrieved from https://www.upwork.com/hiring/for-clients/post-mortem-why-we-test/

Slack (2015, April 6). Integrations 101: Adding Twitter to Slack. Retrieved from https://slackhq.com/integrations-101-adding-twitter-to-slack-d7a46b5425d0?gi=9f8926ab0efe

Sleeknote (2017, March 14). A beginner's guide to turning Instagram followers into subscribers. Retrieved from https://medium.com/sleeknotes-e-commerce-favorites/a-beginners-guide-to-turning-instagram-followers-into-subscribers-158412468c72

Soojun-Kim Pang, A. (2014, July 19). Rules for a successful digital sabbatical. Retrieved from https://medium.com/contemplative-computing/rules-for-a-successful-digital-sabbath-5aafa445e883

Spencer, M. K. (2016, January 10). Peach social network — how social media fails. Retrieved from https://medium.com/@Michael_Spencer/peach-social-network-how-social-media-fails-12e9e40261ba

Spurvey, C. (2016, December 23). How I grew my email list using LinkedIn (and now Medium). Retrieved from https://medium.com/your-brand/how-i-grew-my-email-list-using-linkedin-and-now-medium-9e8985e0477b

Stearns, J. (2016, May 27). How journalists build and break trust with their audience online. Retrieved from https://medium.com/1st-draft/how-journalists-build-and-break-trust-with-their-audience-online-9f6938b28479

Stearns, J. (2017, January 4). A roadmap to the best journalism of 2016. Retrieved from https://medium.com/@jcstearns/a-roadmap-to-the-best-journalism-of-2016-7ae929207b97

Suleman, K. (2016, February 24). Has your agency been using Instagram influencers wrong? Retrieved from http://www.prweek.com/article/1384456/agency-using-instagram-influencers-wrong

Tandem (2016, April 6). Marketing under the influence: Social media superstars as a marketing channel. Retrieved from https://medium.com/@TandemCapital/marketing-under-the-influence-social-media-superstars-as-a-marketing-channel-c8db4523588d

ThePensters (2015, December 15). An in-depth manual on how to write a research paper. Retrieved from https://medium.com/@ThePensters/an-in-depth-manual-on-how-to-write-a-research-paper-5b7a59a2f8f3

Troiano, M. (2016, May 11). How do you start writing online? Retrieved from https://byrslf.co/how-do-you-start-writing-online-9a6fb3ef1f8a?gi=8e5a3624e40e

United States Census Bureau (2017). American Fact Finder: Community facts. Retrieved from https://factfinder.census.gov/faces/nav/jsf/pages/index.xhtml

Van Rooy, D. (2015, January 14). BSQ: The only goal-setting framework you will ever need. Retrieved from https://www.inc.com/david-van-rooy/the-only-goal-setting-framework-you-will-ever-need.html

Vaynerchuk, G. (2016, May 17). My thesis on how to handle feedback. Retrieved from https://medium.com/@garyvee/my-thesis-on-how-to-handle-feedback-d385406fcaf

Vijayashanker, P. (2015, October 27). Self-publishing: A series of experiments + endless self-promotion. Retrieved from https://artplusmarketing.com/self-publishing-a-series-of-experiments-endless-self-promotion-7890e659d3ba

Vijayashanker, P. (2016, June 2). Feedback got you in a frenzy? Learn how to filter it. Retrieved from https://medium.com/@poornima/feedback-got-you-in-a-frenzy-learn-how-to-filter-it-4ee1ef5e0d99

Wilkerson, D. (2013, August 19). How often should I post on Facebook or Twitter? Retrieved from http://www.lunametrics.com/blog/2013/08/19/frequency-post-facebook-twitter/

Williams, N. (2016, October 19). How to welcome feedback (advice from a fellow perfectionist). Retrieved from https://medium.com/@envycollect/how-to-welcome-feedback-advice-from-a-fellow-perfectionist-bc81b58c9ca2

Yeung, T. (2016, December 16). 7 popular fashion contests of this week: Pinterest marketing showcase. Retrieved from https://medium.com/@tkwyoung/7-popular-fashion-contents-of-this-week-pinterest-marketing-showcase-7e6c4f34af10

Zhou, A. (2016, May 16). Mastering influencer marketing: 9 key questions and answers. Retrieved from https://news.greylock.com/how-to-master-influencer-marketing-9-key-questions-and-answers-c14ff728d6a5

Zorzini, C. (2016, October 24). SemRush vs Ahrefs vs SpyFu vs Majestic vs Moz. Retrieved from https://medium.com/@zorzini/semrush-vs-ahrefs-vs-spyfu-vs-majestic-vs-moz-ddc035b53dda

Made in the USA
Middletown, DE
10 August 2023

36499198R00104